Arise
Peace to Heal

Arise
Peace to Heal

Trishan P Kaur

Marketed by

NIYOGI
BOOKS

Printed and Marketed by

NIYOGI BOOKS

D-78, Okhla Industrial Area, Phase-I
New Delhi-110 020, India
Tel: 91-11-26816301, 49327000
Fax: 91-11-26810483, 26813830
email: niyogibooks@gmail.com
www.niyogibooks.com

ISBN: 978-93-81523-01-8
Year of Publication: 2011

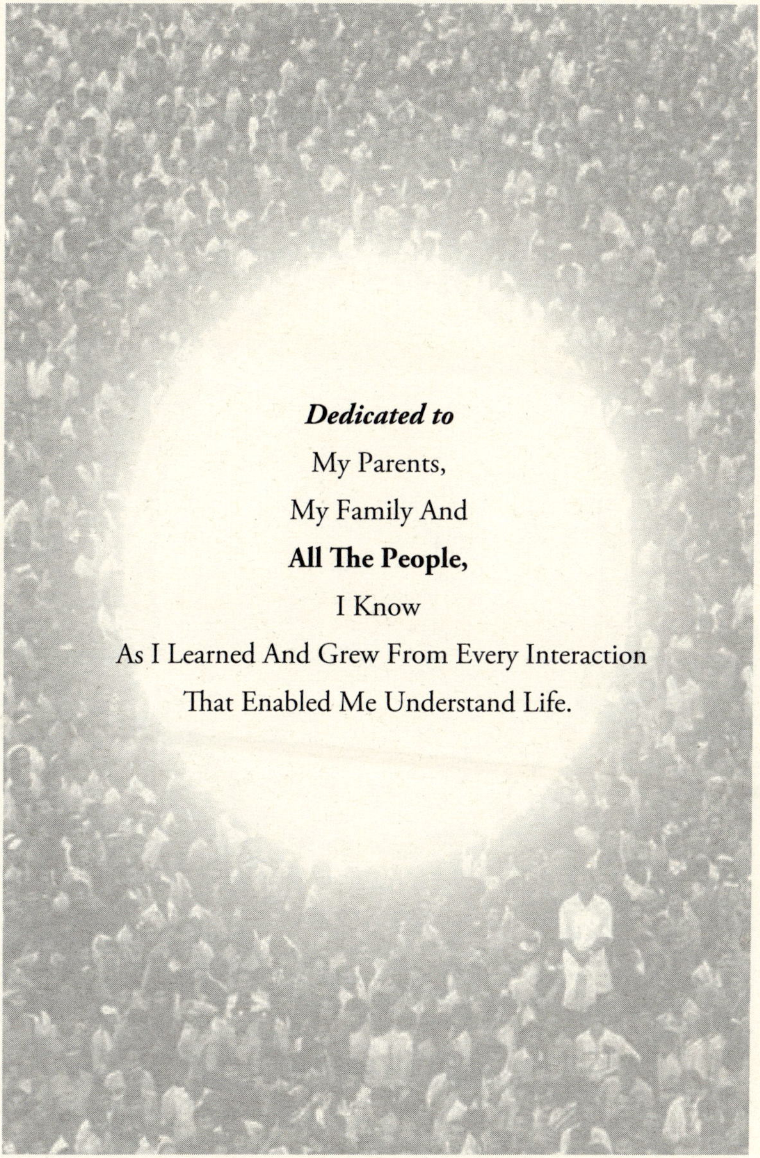

Dedicated to

My Parents,

My Family And

All The People,

I Know

As I Learned And Grew From Every Interaction

That Enabled Me Understand Life.

What a Riddle of Life!*

It has confused all the minds,
Everyone seeks it all through life,
Some say, it's only a thought,
And a word in the mind...

I can tell you about mine
It's my life's delight...
And always in my sight...
I enjoy it day and night.

It goes to sleep,
In the dark night...
It shines in the day,
In the bright sunlight...

It comes along with life,
Within, child crying...
It's quiet and stays with you,
Till the end of life...

It cannot be there,
When justice is blind...
It comes to all equally,
With freedom of time...

It lies deep,
Resting in the sea,
Under the tides...
It is in the sky,
With stars twinkling behind...

Violence and war are unable to find,
It cannot stay with those,
Whose behavior is snide ...

---

* See Answer on page 5

A war in the front,
And a war behind,
It's in their middle,
We say it's _____* time.

Ask, the souls and your minds,
They do not want war but _____* hives,
Only _____*, can keep life alive.

It is not only a word,
It needs to be created and cared,
It's always plenty to be shared,

Don't lose it,
With violence outside,
And violence in the mind,

It gives you health,
It gives you life,
It holds the freedom and pleasure of mind.

It nurtures the nature,
It's giving all the time,
It's a blessing for all life,

It's lying unconscious,
In every mind...
That you have to arise,

Everywhere, it's laying...
And playing, the game of life.
You can always find,
When you are kind...

---

*See Answer on page 5

It's every human's right,

Only, we need to be wise,
And have a thought kind,
It will come to you
Getting delight, delight, delight...

You will see it arise,
When you light your conscious,
With justice and love,
And the good will for all life...

It will heal your body and mind
Awakening your spirit, it will rise,
Showering happiness and harmony in your life...

No crime and no fight,
Will touch your life,
You will live a peaceful life.

ACKNOWLEDGEMENTS

Thanks, millions of millions - - -
To the Creator!
Who gave me 'Human life'!
For all the life's Virtues - - -
And Blessings - - -
Topped with 'Peace Divine'!
For blessing me 'Insight'- - -
And 'Understanding',
To write this book - - -
"Arise Peace to Heal"!

I am indebted to my parents, brother, sister, husband, children, other family members and friends, connected to my life, whose unstinted love and care strengthened me and nourished my mind that filled my life with joy and pride.

I respect Dr. Anu George and Dr. M.P.S. Gandhi as dedicated noble professionals, for their knowledge and opinion and thank them to have spared time to go through the various parts of the book, especially the chapter "Arise Peace to Heal", highlighting the relationship of peace to health.

I appreciate their sincere spirit of cooperation and thank Mr. Haridas for editing the book, Mr. S.S. Negi, Mrs. Suchitra Roy for developing ideas for the cover page and graphics designer Mr Shaju K Anthony. I am also very grateful to Mr Bikas Niyogi for arranging for the book's publication.

I am thankful to all the people, who helped me accomplish, the task of writing and presenting this book to everyone. I would like to particularly thank Manish, Zed, Noor, Amarjit, Surinder, Simar, Reema, Prateek, Arshad, Harris, Harikala and S. P. Mahajan. I would also like to express my heartfelt thanks to all my near and dear ones, who participated directly or indirectly and helped with their own special touch and time in creation of peace, through this book, "Arise Peace to Heal".

Big Thanks to big people, Mr. Bill Gates, Larry Page and Sergey Brin, enriching all with knowledge through MS word and Google, the writing tools and world window to knowledge respectively, for which I could accomplish the task of writing so easily and present the complex ideas in a simple and straight forward manner.

CONTENTS

PROLOGUE

I missed my connecting flight to U.S. at Heathrow airport due to late arrival of flight from Indonesia. As I had long wait for next possible flight, I walked down the hallway to find waiting lounge. I looked around for a good spot and some company while I entered the lounge. There, I spotted an impressive lady wearing a beautiful dress who was sitting alone and some chairs were lying vacant adjacent to her and I went down to sit next to her. I introduced myself and she said hello adjusting her bag; she told me that she was Jazara, passenger from another flight. Sitting together for a while we watched TV and had some intermittent conversation. She told me that her flight was also delayed due to some technical snag; and there was no clue how long repair would take and both of us had long waiting for our next flights.

After chatting and watching TV for about an hour we planned to walk around and check out prices at duty free shops. None of us was interested in buying anything as it turned out nothing was of particular interest to either of us. After passing through a few shops, we decided to retire into some quiet corner. We went to café and found a table with comfortable seats by side of the door. It was almost like a corner and we planned to spend our time to relax in that cozy spot. Jazara got a cold coffee and I got mocha with extra chocolate. View outside was very clear from our table and it was interesting to see how everyone was rushing through corridors dragging their bags...

Jazara commented, "Look, how everyone is running through terminals, as if unaware of anything else around them!"

I looked at her enquiringly and asked, "What do you mean?"

"Oh! Nothing; Just that...", Jazara said after a pause, "I am trying to understand people and fast track life in today's world.

"Yes, everyone seems to be short of time, running fast like running machines! You know doctors say our bodies are like machines. Could we call ourselves "Human robots", "What do you say?"

"Human robots"! Robots don't have sensitivity like living beings and they work without any consciousness. Perhaps human beings are becoming robots too...quite insensitive and ignorant about other human beings.

"Is that true? Are people becoming machines? No more feelings for humans and humanity!"

"Where is humanity?" said Jazara with wet eyes and choked voice. "It is vanishing with every passing day...-"

I looked at her quietly.

After remaining silent for couple of minutes, Jazara calmed down and told how her elder sister was killed in 9/11 terrorist attack and uncertainty of life of her family members and friends at her father's village due to bombing from war in that area. She narrated all horrible tales of violence and suffering, her loving family members and friends had to undergo for no fault of theirs...-

It was time for us to part ways now; we exchanged emails and said good-bye to each other. Jazara left a deep impact of her suffering and pain on me. My impressions of war and terrorism tired me more than my entended journey time, due to mismanaged flights...I reached home quite late and went to prepare my bed and left my luggage unpacked. Tired from the journey and the impressions of violence from Jazara's painful experiences..., I went to sleep with the hope to see an end to people suffering from violence...The dark night was turbulent and blind as if there were dark clouds over sky, with thundering wars and violence dancing high...

I don't remember when 'fairy of Peace' embraced me in arms... perhaps took me to 'heaven of peace' in deep slumber; there were no worries, no sufferings...only peace, peace and peace...

*Answer:

It is a heavenly delight,
People seek it life after life,
This is PEACE and its might.
It can be in every mind's sight,
And 'Delight' of every life.

---

* for-***What a Riddle of Life!***

_____= peace

INTRODUCTION

Today peace seems to have been trampled over by rising violence with some evil design in human life. All round escalation of violence has put life to hard times. People have sick bodies and restless minds. Along with violence, disease is on rise. There seems no end to misery of disease in body and violence in life. Evil violence has knocked out peace with malice towards life that has to be understood by every mind. Arising and rising peace high is the only way to end all misery and pain caused by violent strife.

This book is my attempt of a tiny effort about strengthening Peace and Harmony in life. What is peace? How does peace matter to human beings? Why we need to create peace? How to create peace in life? Sharing my ideas through this book is sincere concern for each individual and wish to see peace blowing through every mind. I have tried to present a simple and an understandable way to cultivate peace and harmony.

Since violence has been glorified by vested interests, peace has become riddle of life. People undermine its value and lack understanding about its importance in their living and life. Violence of terror and war coupled with corruption and social injustice has humbled peace in hands of devils and beasts. Therefore, to disengage people from violence, understanding of peace and its values for individual health and harmony is very important.

How peace is toppled by our own minds and a thought choice that results into violent actions, fights and crime? How do social injustice, corruption and other vices create fertile ground for violence and it propagates through social crime? Terror and war create violence in mind that destroys our health and disrupts peace of our life. How important are justice and other virtues to build not only social peace but also your own health and harmony in life? How important is virtuous habit of our mind to achieve health and happiness in life?

All types of thoughts confuse our minds until we know wrong and right. Peace in thoughts is only right choice because it is essential for a healthy body and harmony in life. Peace exists in dormant stage in subconscious, until individual decides to make choice of peace consciously and it becomes a habit of mind. Building educated understanding is a way to make a correct choice. We have to give recognition and acceptance to thoughts of peace over violence and war and make it our thought choice.

An interesting 'peace formula' to develop understanding of peace and peaceful behavior has been propounded in the book, for individual as well as social peace at any level in life. 'Peace formula', in equation form, is simple guide to achieve peace in all walks of life. Importance of components of peace has been explained through poems and text that can interest a wider audience and be helpful to people from all ages and stages in developing understanding of peace.

How important are our individual thoughts and our choices in creating peace and violence? What is impact of violence and peace on disease and health in human body? How does mind with thoughts of peace and violence, interact with brain and impacts body physiology, effecting development of disease and healing process? How is mind involved in emotional, behavioral, spiritual and social health of human being? How important families and schools can be in training minds of children in developing peaceful behaviors and creation of social peace?

Peaceful behavior is an individual responsibility and the guideline to achieve the same is given for all adorable children who seek to do something about improving life and bringing about social change. Blessed will be they with a healthy body and peaceful life and their future will welcome them with success and happiness all the time, who arise peace in their behavior and mind.

I seek to lighten...
Peace in every mind,
Turn souls and hearts kind,
'Power of peace' to every young mind,

May their hands hold destiny of their choice,
And their heads held high,
May their minds be victorious with peaceful might!
May God bless them ...

With 'His,' power and might.
To defeat vicious evil,
In its violent design ...

Longing and desire for peace comes to each individual naturally as that is driven by desire for integration of individual's self and with the other human beings that is true value and nature of peace. Peace is first of five essential elements that constitute life. Each life must maintain an essential peace balance for vitality and healthy functioning of it's life systems. Therefore peace is an essential need and we must arise and rise peace to heal disease and develop harmony and health in life.

The book 'Arise peace to heal' would shake up conscious of people and dissuade them from corruption of mind, vices and violence. It will help to build individual health and promote healthy living and social harmony. No one can escape fire of violence that can only be cooled with peace in minds for that we need to strengthen ethics in life that will bring about integrity to people's character and values of peace like justice and equal rights that will contribute to integration of humanity, bestowing health and well being to all humankind.

Peace is latent divine energy that imparts us health and vitality. It is need of people, who have sick bodies and stressed minds and those who fail to recognize the disruption of peace, through aggression and violence of their behavior in everyone's life. They need to read this book 'Arise peace to heal' and educate their minds with peace and its values to make peace a choice and habit of their mind for better health and peaceful behavior, promoting harmony and happiness in everyones life.

KNIGHT OF THE RIGHT

After a long peaceful night,
I woke up in the morning light,
Enveloped in tranquility and quiet,
I saw a bright light...
As if peace was radiating from that light...
Was it 'Divine might' and 'peace light'?
Where, Peace was in sight...
My plight is for no fight...
Dawn of the day, asked quietly...
You be a 'Knight' of the 'Right'...
"Light your heart", a voice was saying,
Blessed you are; with 'His' might...
See Thy Light smiling so bright...
There is DELIGHT, DELIGHT, and DELIGHT...

Lying mesmerized, I was listening to a sweet voice, when a sudden cool breeze rattled the blinds. Slowly I turned and moved towards the window. My eyes scanned whole room searching for the sweet voice…

Drawing a blank, I recalled its sweet tone…

Casting aside my lethargy, rubbing eyes off their sleep ... I got up and leaned on pillow while trying to sit down...

I shook my head and mind, immersed in the sweet voice...I pinched my hand and woke up my mind, to see where the sweet voice was blowing from ... I opened my eyes...looked around... everywhere was blank and dark... I was unable to find...

Ah! It was all a dream! ...I realized, as my mind awakened.

Amused and surprised, I went back to bed, but my ears were busy listening... soft squawks, whistles, fluttering and chirping sounds...

Quickly, I jumped out of bed...a thought flashed across my mind... maybe it's there! ...the voice that was calling!

I walked up to window and saw an old tree, crowded with couples of cuckoos, swifts and parrots; fluttering their wings, hopping and hovering over branches, chattering with each other in their chirpy and squeaky voices. Hustle and bustle of birds threw wild guesses into my mind about their ongoing activity...

... are birds playing?
... might be dancing!
... may be they are doing morning exercises!
... might be having celebration!
... might be planning their day!
... might be assigning tasks to each other!
... are they in for a meeting?

Whatever it was, they were welcoming the new day. It seemed as if they were celebrating the new beginning of life at the dawn of a new day. It was a lovely scene! Happiness and energy seemed to be floating in the air like 'melody of wind' as if sung by a bird in her squeaks filled with delight. They were teeming with life and its moments of happiness, fluttering their wings incessantly, hopping over to each other; turning their necks vigilantly, flashing small shining eyes swiftly, moving all around. Enthusiasm was evident in each of them, as if they were ready to take on great tasks lying ahead for the day.

Suddenly a loud chi-chi-chi... began!

What is that?

Out of nowhere, pandemonium erupted; suddenly all squeaks and chirpy noises became louder. I looked around to find out what caused birds voices get louder.

Wow! beautiful sunrise left me spellbound! I understood the secret of 'rejoicing birds', sun had just begun to arise. It was the magic of golden sunrays that created a fresh "spell of life" and cool morning air infused liveliness in environment. As if electrified, the birds seemed to be bursting with energy and excitement.

Sunrise is Nature's wake up call, it lights up the day with sunshine, renews and rejuvenates life with sun's warmth showered on all creation, driving away darkness of the night gone by. Bemused, I took a few deep breaths to get some clean and fresh morning air and felt as if a stream of energy blew inside and I thanked God for all 'His' blessings and gifts of life.

Elation and excitement took over my dullness and lethargy. It seemed as if I had imbued happiness and energy of birds. Full of joy, I felt like jumping, flying, shouting and running around; free and wild like birds...I wished if, only I could change myself into small birdie and climb up tree to join enjoying birds and able to talk to them!

Incoming breeze tickled me, sending chill through body with that I moved from window to go inside. Doused in happiness and amusement, I thanked birds for this morning treat...waking me up with their sweet squeaks...

It was indeed a wonderful morning! With freshness of first blush of new day, everything seemed to have turned new and more beautiful. Happy and excited, I started getting ready to go out for a walk.

I looked through newspaper headlines, as I was getting ready... A harrowing editorial headline of the newspaper said ...

"WAR FOR ACHIEVING PEACE"

Huh...! What does that mean? War for peace... What? It sounds so absurd! ...One contradicts the other!

How's one possible in presence of other?

Contradictory headline kept flashing across my eyes...while I was shuffling through newspaper pages, wondering if it was – - -a piece of 'mockery of Peace' or an action of violence was their treat?

'War bugles' buzzed through my joyous mind...

An alert knocked on my conscious, shaking out thoughts, charged with worries of violence that can bring destruction, disease, pain and misery in people's life...

As violence started gripping my mind, I skipped reading the editorial and put the newspaper aside. Picking up the keys, I got out of the house. While I passed through the driveway, on to the sidewalk, I saw the War Memorial Park just across the road and headed there for my morning walk.

A serene and quiet environment in the War Memorial Park took away all the worries of mind. Through remnants of war scene left behind from the past war, I looked around to find clue to the kind of 'war for peace' might had been designed...what a war can do, for peace in life?

WAR FOR ACHIEVING PEACE

As I walked down the War Memorial Park, the newspaper headline "WAR FOR ACHIEVING PEACE" started flashing in front of my eyes again and again. Buzzing 'bugles of war' threw my mind into worries of cruelty and misery it can bring along...

I remembered Jazara, who showed her pain and suffering caused by violence of war and terrorism. My mind tried to dig up the history of war that was showing its remnants at the Memorial Park. Newspaper headline was foretelling another war-- - Along with that impending war, scene of the Memorial Park, raised scenes of war from past times...

Picture of loss of life, in war memorial, pricked my mind that started throwing up questions... Had this war been fought to achieve peace? Did this war achieve peace?

Leaving war and peace down, I climbed up a small hill to view the whole park. It was a big park with lots of trees and roads, passing through memory stones of war heroes. There were only a few people in park. Once in a while someone came and stood by a tombstone, probably paying homage, or trying to overcome their loneliness with memories of their departed loved ones.

It was a cool and chilly morning, waiting for sunrays to warm up the day. Sun was very bright but sunshine was still not warm enough. Without a jacket it was rather cold and the tall old trees kept sunshine away from most of park area. I tried to cut through shady stretches moving towards sunny area, walking briskly to warm up myself...

Suddenly a woman passed by with big scary dog that frightened me, dog looked ferocious and was without leash. Later I noticed, the dog was so disciplined and when the woman stopped by a tombstone, neither did the dog move nor made any noise. As long as the woman stood by the tombstone, the dog kept standing with its head bowed down as if participating in prayers.

I wondered about that woman and other people engrossed in deep thoughts in quiet vicinity of the tombstones.

Did they really derive any consolation in company of lifeless stones? Those tombstones were just like any stone, lying here and there or used in construction … least capable of sharing anyone's grief.

"How were these people so connected to the stones?" I wondered.

I kept looking around curiously and watching people in amazement….

Soon I realized, while I was trying to understand the equation of stones with people, those stones were not just chunks of ordinary stones used dispassionately to erect buildings. Those stones were special because each of them represented a 'special soul', whose touch reverberated through stone making it special. Those tombstones represented loving touch of sincere and powerful emotions of loving people, connected through emotional chord with departed souls. They now reverberate with love, providing touch of warmth and solace to loved ones left behind. Now I could relate anew to people praying at tombstones and admired their sincere love and I prayed for solace and peace of their minds.

The stones 'stood in silence'! Perhaps each person standing alongside stones conversed mutely with the souls. Peace was a silent spectator to union of souls in presence of beautiful Nature, where intruders like me passed by...

"Why was I so touched for those people?" I questioned myself. .

None of them were my concern, but I still felt deeply involved and my heart cried and reached out to them. I indulged in wish ful thinking... if only I could change things for them, bring their loved ones back…

Heaving a sigh, I looked around and saw two women walking by, who broke into a jog. I followed them as I realized that I had slowed down, I started walking briskly to finish it early as I had planned to take up all the pending work at home today.

As I continued my walk, people by tomb stones were still on my mind, pondering over their loneliness and loss of their loved ones, who got killed in war and my mind wanted to ask them... did you get peace in life, with this war of your time?

While on one hand, natural beauty and lively park were very pleasant but its mournful, dichotomous scene of sad memories was upsetting that stirred in sadness in my mind and my heart missed a beat every time, while I saw a sad person standing by a tombstone. Like ocean's spring tides on moonlit night, questions started raking in my mind as editorial headline flashed in front of my eyes...

"WAR FOR ACHIEVING PEACE!"

War for Peace!!
Peace from War!! Peace from Violence?
What does it mean!
What is War? What is Violence?
What is Peace?
How did these people feel, when they died?
Did these people like violence and fight?
Did they not like Peace?
How does any War happen?
What causes people to fight and be violent?
What does anyone get out of Violence?
Can anything be good about Violence?
Should Violence have approval of civilized mankind?
Should violence be acceptable in civilized world?
Is there any way to end violence and War? ...

Endless questions about violence and war stirred my mind, churning through all peace and inertia, causing pandemonium and darkness...I looked up above...calling to 'Divine'... flashed hope for peace with golden streaks of sunshine... elated my mind as I walked through an open lane with bright sunlight...

Sudden buzzing followed me and buzzing bugles echoed 'war cries' as I noticed a bee passed by my right ear... sounding my mind. With a bewildered mind, I gazed up through trees as "war... peace" headline, flashed back ... Thinking resolutely, determined to find answers, I glanced at the people standing by stones and looked at each tomb stone, reading names; with a teetering hope for clues... looking for answers to questions raking my mind...

I got it! Suddenly my mind hit upon something...it seemed to have been catching up some clues!...

What do we get out of war? ...Seemed to be answered!

As if shouts came from the tombs..., all souls around me screamed..., through their 'deathly silence and stillness', lying lifeless in lap of "Mother Earth"... All lives ended into death that are now buried under these tombstones! ...souls engulfed by silence followed me, while I was entangled in deliberations... I concentrated on each tomb, I felt each soul had materialized, emerging silently from its tomb saying, "I got death."

Deathly silence, spreading all around, was gripping my mind!

"We got Death out of War," souls seemed to scream through their tombs that dipped into silence... as if it also gripped everything outside...

The cemetery was depicting death and destruction brought about by Violence in the past. An end to human lives resulted on both sides of battle; regardless, who won it or who had lost.

In an intense confabulate, with souls, I heard ...they were saying something more as they went back, leaving behind total stillness and deep silence!

What...? I could not get it.

Wait...! I tried to stop souls, in an effort to understand them...

"I got Peace!"... Saying that last soul disappeared back into its silent abode.

'Peace' dawned all around as the souls' departed..., Ah! Silence and Peace!

These souls were put to rest in 'deep silence and peace'!

I sighed in relief and tried to rest my mind with thoughts of peace that had got embroiled in violence and silence, in memorial park with story of War, Death and Peace...I turned up my hand to see the time and continued to walk...

In no time, my mind got restless and started juggling questions of War, Death and peace, exciting my mind that was at ease... 'silence of the beautiful park, bedding sleeping souls in their restful peace got disrupted by two crows fighting for a bread piece'...

Shaking away violence, I treaded through the peace zone of the park, full of blooming flowers and green leaves on thick trees... the amused mind started delving into the mystery of life and creation by the Almighty...

How life is infused into every living being, and then taken away just like that?

Story of life and living is same for all... but death comes differently to every living being. This knotty mystery is beyond human understanding... Lost in mystery of life and death, I continued my walk...

While I was enjoying moments of life and lively environment,

I could not ignore War and Peace. Here, violence had ended so many lives-

Did this war get any peace?

“Did souls escape from violence to silence or did violence put them to silence?”...Questions pricked my mind! ...

Editorial headline “WAR FOR ACHIEVING PEACE” flashed again and again, blinding my eyes with its glaring and agonizing notification... the only solution for achieving ‘PEACE’ was endorsed with approval of violence –

All I could see at the park...Violence, Destruction and Death!

...where is Peace?

A dog barking near a statue of a war hero diverted my mind to the war memorial and again it picked up remnants of the violence around me...

May be this ‘silence of souls’ is peace!

War! ... past war, perhaps that may have been fought for peace!

I researched for ‘peace’, in ‘war - the violence’...only ‘death’ could be seen ...

Had souls been drowned by violence or did they escape to silence?

Is it violence or peace! There is only violence...No peace!!

Souls...! Silence...! No life...! It cannot be my peace!

From roadside, barks of a dog, caught my attention, disrupting my thought commune with souls..., my mind became quiet and there was 'silence and peace'. ...Ah some 'PEACE'! ...'Peace' in this war and death's seat!

My mind was now at ease,...it tried to untangle War, Death and Peace,... different ends of the strands of violence and peace, causing confusion...

How that can be peace?
Death is the only way to this Peace!
Is Peace inherent in Death and Violence only?

If violence is approved for peace, that will bring every human to doorway of death to get his peace! That means there has to be a violence, and subsequent deaths, to bring Peace anywhere. ...everyone one has to be violent and fight war!

Violence…! everywhere, everyone at war (violence) ...Ha! Ha! Ha! ...Violence should be rule of life!... wait for death to bring Peace! Death to all people! ...left only dead bodies!

No one will be alive! There will be no human life!

Total silence and Peace! ...

Where are souls? ...Searching...Cannot find them!

Where are bodies? ...Searching...Can find only ashes, no bodies!

Oh, God! So horrifying...is this Peace? 'Peace!'- Composed of 'ashes of life'!...searching for souls...where are souls?

I cannot find as there is no more human life......No life left behind!

Who will witness this peace? ONLY GHOSTS WOULD BE THERE!! NO HUMANKIND!!

Dreams of Peace in life, seemed crumbling with 'violent dance' of violence!

Dancing "Yama of Death" seemed snatching dreams of any life in peace on earth.

"No! That could not be right"!

Violence is not the path to achieve peace. We get only violence out of Violence, not any peace. God did not create us all to go to war - violence and die. In spite of so much violence, Peace still eludes us.

I slowed down near a flagpole to enjoy colorful flower beds. Lively and pleasing flowers, filled my heart with joy...again, I started my walk with elated mood...

It is amazing, how life all around in nature met death below.... It was like an exhibition of God's wonder of creation and annihilation. While I was brooding over this dual mystery of life, suddenly a speeding car honked, on road adjacent to park and shook me out of my muddled thoughts...

Enjoying intermittent sunlight with a cool breeze, I looked up through the trees...

The bright sunrays filtered in through the leaves...
With every golden ray, lighting...
A renewed hope for peace...
The 'peace' that is life's feast...
The 'peace' that greets and meets humanity,
The 'vibrant Peace',
That goes with life on its wheels.
Flying on the wings of health,
With a healthy glow and a happy sheen...
As if lighting...
...the face, of 'Peace Queen'!

DAY OF PEACE

At the end of the day, I sat down to relax and logged on to computer, to solve some puzzles and write mail to my parents. I looked through news, enjoyed reading some funny cartoons and jokes and tried on some painting. I was about to log off when I received Jazara's email. She wrote about well-being of her family and sent me a couple of pages that she had written for her teaching assignments. These were pages from her recollections of some of her life's eventful days. She didn't talk about her writings during our airport meeting and this was real surprise for me. I started reading her email curiously...

"How wonderful can be peace? I realized it the day after I moved to my new house, wrote Jazara. My first independent house brought a 'day of peace', like a 'day of life'. I want to capture it forever."...

It was interesting and I continued reading ... To cut short I jumped lines in between and picked Jazara's important thoughts and feelings about peace. After a quick look over I logged off and slouched in my easy chair, to relax for some moments with Jazara's 'day of peace'. My mind picked Jazara's 'thoughts of peace' from her 'day of peace' and started communicating with its own conscious...

"You can live so much more in a 'day of peace'! Every moment of a peaceful day becomes longer and relaxed. It seems as if longevity of day as well as life has increased. You get required break and rest for yourself, more time and, space for yourself that helps to organize yourself and your life."...

"I want to remember it always! ...I want every other day like this because it gives me so much pleasure and contentment," Jazara wrote, "I am writing it so that I can read and live it up, again and again and enjoy pleasure of this day, 'day of peace'..."

A 'day of peace' generates strength insurmountable with multiplied nerve power; mind and body exuberate with energy. The boundless mind gains 'infinite creative power' in freedom of space given by 'peaceful moments' ...

As I was going over Jazara's 'day of peace,' it relaxed me too...and I took a break from the computer to enjoy some peace. After spending a couple of minutes on my rocking chair, enjoying some rest and a dream for everyone's peace...

I got up early as I had slept long, goodnight's sleep in much shorter time. Yesterday's tiredness was blown away as if I was never tired. I could not believe that I am no longer tired in spite of an eventful and hectic previous day. Sourness of my body muscles due to all that weight lifting during our move in, last evening had disappeared. I was fresh and ready to start with first day in new house as if I had long been living in this 'peaceful house' with a 'peaceful environment' ...To take my dog out and know the area better, I got out from the house, to have a stroll in the adjoining park, Green Hill Park...

Suddenly, on road adjacent to park, a car sped away. As I looked across the road, a part of the Hill Square could be seen, where I had lived until yesterday. The inner colony roads were my favorite to take short walks, whenever I got some time...But those roads were not as 'pleasant and peaceful' as these Green Hill Park trails. While living at Hill square, I always searched to seize some 'peace for hurried mind' during walks through busy colony streets. Old memories came fresh in my mind...Anyway forget everything... I shrugged off unpleasant thoughts and started planning the day, Jazara described further...

"Green Hill Park was quiet and full of greenery, 'freshening and rejuvenating'...I thanked God for 'day of peace'... I sighed with relief, remembring days, I stayed with Laqueta* in her brother-in-law Elon's** house...

"Hi there"! ...broke my thoughts. It was Betty,* a friend who worked at nearby grocery store. I often saw her at the store, while shopping.

"Hi Betty," I replied, "How are you?"

Betty said, "I am fine, just walking down to the store."

I have to go shopping and will see you at the store after lunch.

O.K. bye…see ya, said Betty and left on her way.

As Betty passed by, I realized I had been walking for over an hour by now and I headed back to my house. It was unbelievable, I had finished my walk so early and day had yet to start. I looked at sky with hope to finish all the pending tasks today.

On my way back to home, I started counting tasks for the day...After reaching home, I banged on door as I entered Elroy's*** room and stamped my feet to ensure he knew it was time to wake up. To my surprise, Elroy opened his eyes with a big smile.

---

* a friend, ** Laqueta's brother-in-law, ***Jazara's son

Oh! You are awake! I can't believe…

"It's a beautiful morning", Elroy said, "I slept very well last night". He complained, "Why did you make so much noise? I was in a dream…"

"What was your dream?" I asked. ...

"It was a strange place, umm…I can't remember now...I will tell you later, when I remember", said Elroy inconclusively and asked," Where did you go?"

I went out for a walk close by, to Green Hill Park", I told Elroy, you know, Hill Square was visible from park across road on other side, but Elon's house could not be seen from there...

Really! How did you like the Park? Elroy asked.

It is very pleasant and full of lush green trees. Would you like to see it?

Yes, why not!

Why don't you start your day with jog in the park?

No! Not so early! Especially I don't want to miss this pleasant morning...something is greatly different today! Something in this house is very good today...What is it?

Try to guess?

Is it just because it's a new house?

No my darling, it is something much more than that. It is a day, 'full of peace', in 'peaceful house'. There are no tensions and worries of Tavon* and his mom that you had at that old house.

You are right mom! I was feeling relaxed and happy when we moved in here.

I will make you some yummy lemonade if you get out of bed...

Wow! That will be great mom! Agreed, I will get up, cheerfully Elroy said. Fresh lemonade was his favorite drink. Elroy put on some music and got up to brush his teeth...

As I finished making lemonade, Elroy came over humming song in an elated mood and had lemonade.

Yummy! Cheerful Elroy said with brightened eyes as he started sipping lemonade, It had never tasted like this before.

I always make it like this and it has the same taste.

Then why does it taste different today? asked Elroy.

I smiled, Oh! That's because you are so 'happy and relaxed' for this new wonderful day, in this peaceful house."

Yes, it feels so different today; everything seems so good, I feel so light and totally relaxed. I don't have to worry about anything, said Elroy.

---

*Son of Laqueta

I felt happy to see Elroy so cheerful and relieved of tense environment he had to live through for the past few days.

After sitting quietly for a few moments, Elroy said, Mom I don't understand Elon* and Adara's** evil behavior towards Tavon and his mom. Their actions and language were so tasteless and downright awful. No one would believe that they are so highly qualified after seeing their undignified and insulting behavior. What sort of professor is Elon, who did not hesitate to use uncouth language? If I felt so bad how would have Tavon and his mom felt?

I tried to pacify Elroy by saying that even I couldn't understand their behavior. He used to be upset and wanted to interfere to help and cheer Tavon.

Did you get any lessons out of that?

Yes, never go and stay with any family member, as they don't treat you well, Elroy replied bitterly, never trust anyone, except your own mom, dad, sister or brother.

...I don't agree with you. Everyone is not like Elon and his family. Aren't Tavon and his mom nice? Your own house is always more comfortable with all the freedom for you...but living jointly with someone has its own advantages; ... it varies from person to person; it is not difficult to work things out a better way, where people understand each other and give equal importance to each other's needs...you can enjoy more with more people...Imagine, if only Jenny*** had behaved better with Tavon how different would have been things...

---

* Laqueta's brother-in-law , **Laqueta's sister-in-law, ***Laqueta's niece

May be you are right, mom.

We should not to do their wrongs ourselves; we should take care of our own actions and behavior and forget about them. I am proud of you for being such a nice and wise son...The most important thing for you to learn is that you can pass through hardest of circumstances with flying colors. Didn't you see how tolerant and focused was Tavon?

You are right mom. I will always concentrate on my work and won't get involved in nasty things, said Elroy.

--Will you please get ready now? We have got a lot to do today.

...Umm! It feels so cool! Let's talk some more, I feel like talking today...It was hard to get this day!"

I'm happy too, for this 'day of peace'. We will talk later. We have the whole day with us.

Mom, Please!

Idea!* Let's celebrate today as a 'day of Peace' so that we can always remember it.

That sounds great! Yay...! We'll celebrate our 'day of Peace'. Peace celebration, saying that Elroy started jumping and dancing...

A day, of 'celebration of Peace'...

---

* Now, I understood Jazara's idea and her longing for peace...

LIFE GOES ON

A 'day of peace', is only a couple of hours of peace that is enough to recuperate and rebound body with strength and energy. How peace brings back balance and order in life, organizing actions of mind that controls life through control of our actions and maintaining balance and harmony in life? That's amazing!

Why is it so hard to find peace? How does it vanish from our mind? Can it survive with man in his civilized life? Can all of us beget it in our life? Does it hide somewhere? ...I must try to find. Where does it reside? ...inside or outside! Where should I find? ...In house or in people's minds! I have to catch it, even if it hides from my sight.

Let me start with life, it may know peace more than I. ...Perhaps life is an 'action' of actions that goes on and on...and life goes on with its 'action for life'...Jazara writes...A home and a family, everyone has to find, to undertake journey of life...one, I found mine at Newtown...a home or a house, I could not define...Is there anything mine? These are puzzles of life! ... A family, relationship ties and people, life in a home or outside... somewhere peace resides! I have to begin search from my house and family... Peace, I have to find, writes Jazara...

A HOUSE

I had just moved to Newtown and Laqueta was first person, whom I met at local library, where I had gone in search of job. As I had to make some queries, I went to reference desk, to ask for help from Laqueta. She not only sweetly explained to me all about library and people who worked there, she helped my instant placement. Later in the day, we happened to have lunch breaks at same time.

While I was exchanging tips with Laqueta, she suddenly stopped talking! She couldn't speak and was turning red; I realized she was choking. Quickly, I jumped from my seat and gave her a 'push of life,' clearing out a piece of apple stuck in her windpipe. She was really touched and became emotional; hugging me she said crying, "You are Godsend for me." I was happy that I could act timely to help her and thanked God for giving me the insight and courage in moment of urgency and need. We became friends from that very moment.

Laqueta had a son Tavon, about my son's age and he too was staying with her. She told me that she had recently moved from Texas and was living as a paying guest with her brother in law, Elon. She had been living with Elon's family for about two months now. She told me all about her family and hassels of getting visa for United States..

While we were talking, she hinted about a room to be let out by Elon. That became really easy for me, as I was new at Newtown. The room I rented out was adjoining Laqueta's room but it had an independent access from the backyard. By the weekend, I moved in to new accommodation; and this helped me settle down quickly. As we lived together and worked together, Laqueta and I became very close. We discussed our problems and took each other's advice while making important day-to-day decisions. Sometimes Laqueta looked tense but she would just smile on my enquiring about her mood. Once I found her working absent mindedly, engrossed in some deep thoughts; I felt she wasn't her normal self so I started talking to her. This time she accepted that she was mulling over a problem. I asked her to share it with me. Maybe together we could find a solution and that day, after we got home she gave me her diary to read...

Laqueta wrote, ...It was so cumbersome to get US visas. A lot of paper work was involved and going to embassy again and again with new paper work, was a hell of a task. We never wanted to move from Indonesia as we were doing very well there. It was not easy to wind up everything in Indonesia; hectic running around for visas, dealing with Tavon for going to a new school ...It was difficult. Reluctantly we decided to go through everything for sake of Tavon, for his studies and better career options.

We were so 'glad and mad' after landing at our first destination, Texas. Such a vast country; my God; so many high rise buildings and confusing flyovers ... we were lost in confusion, we felt on land out of this world... perhaps a dreamland...about which, we never imagined.... No wonder everyone dreams of coming to America!

Living in Texas was wonderful experience. People were very nice and helpful. We came across people from different countries and cultures with different languages but didn't face any problems in settling there, although it was new place for us. We enjoyed every bit of our life there, tasting and eating new goodies, making new friends and shopping in malls. Sitting in the library was our favorite pastime. Tavon was especially happy, as the learning experience at school was much better than what he was used to in previous school. Friendly teachers listened to students patiently and they were allowed freedom to do their work with own creativity and originality. In Texas, Tavon was really happy to be involved in extracurricular activities, for which opportunity did not exist in his previous school.

At the end of one academic year, Tavon and I came to stay with

Elon's family, at Newtown. It was difficult decision to move from Texas, as Tavon didn't want to change his school. He liked his curriculum, school environment, friends, and teachers at Texas and he cried umpteen times to continue in the same school until his graduation.

It was not difficult for me to adjust to any circumstances, if I was by myself. But I was not sure as to how Tavon would adjust as an old incident reminded me of Elon's erratic behavior when Tavon was barely 3 years old. Elon's pet dog had licked Tavon and out of fear he shrieked loudly, pushing dog away. Instead of showing any sympathy towards frightened child, Elon got angry and showed no hesitation in hitting Tavon, showing cruel behavior towards a small child...

Newtown was an old and a small town. Elon's house was in the heart of the town and location was quite convenient for living. Tavon's school was about two miles from Elon's house. Tavon was unhappy, as he didn't like school building. He wasn't satisfied with available credit hours and course structure. Out of those courses, he had to study couple of courses by himself without tutoring or guidance. He was upset, wondering if he would be able to maintain his top ranking in class with so much difference in courses and credits in Newtown school. He was anxious about teachers; how helpful would they be? Would he get same friendly environment as in previous school? Would he find some friendly peers? Worried Tavon kept asking these questions.

You are hard working and so concerned about your studies; I am sure you are going to excel in this school too, as you did in previous school. I said, "Don't worry everything will be O.K."I was sure his fears were unfounded because it was a new and unknown situation and he felt out of place. It was very normal for a child of his age to think like that everything looks uncertain in new situation. It was always hard for him to accept change and he took time to adjust. I said, "Be brave and confident, you will be the one, at the top of your class, given your dedication and hard work."... I am sure there must be some good teachers here in Newtown, who will be helpful to you and will care for you. You will definitely reach your goals even now. Though the route you must take may be different from what you planned and expected.

"What if new route looks incredibly difficult?" asked Tavon.

"Leave your worries to God and cheer up" I said, "Will you work harder than you worked in your previous schools?" asked I.

"Why not", said Tavon, "I will work as hard as I can and will not waste my time playing video games."

"Then stop worrying", said I, "am sure you are going to be the best student in school."

Tavon still unable to reconcile said, "But why did God have to change my school?"

"To make you strong", said I. Do you remember, you never wanted to come to America leaving your friends behind? Didn't you find so many new friends in Houston and learned so many new things?"

"You're right Ma, I didn't think of it like that. But I miss all friends and my school. I didn't want to change as I liked it there," said Tavon.

Everything changes in life and Nature; day/night, seasons, summer/ winter…rotating through different stages...Life renews itself through new and different circumstances and we need to keep adjusting opening our minds to the change and working on the requirements of the new situation...

"But I'm still concerned about the new school and teachers – who knows what it will entail?"

"Don't worry, you are not alone?" said I, "I am there to help you. It will not be difficult as there is nothing, that you can't do."

"But I will have to start everything new and I don't know anyone in this school," said Tavon.

I said, "My dear, you will know everyone, once you start going to school."

"You will make friends very soon as all kids are generally nice in schools and everyone likes to have more friends; and teachers love hard working students like you so you should not worry", said I "We may have to lose things we possess and in return we can get new ones. We may have to accept what we don't like as life is not about only what you like."

"But I liked relationships I had built with my friends in Houston. Now I have had to just abandon them, I don't think that is very fair."

“Relationships keep changing like everything else in life, creating new equations with new people and building new relationships is a very important part of living. Life keeps on moving, throwing us into circumstances and we work on changes adjusting ourselves.... I tried to explain to Tavon about some realities of life.

“That’s not good! Why does life change so much?”

“Forget about that is gone and focus on what is in your hands.”

“Yes, mom,” worried Tavon asked, “But how would I manage everything?”

“You know, you always work sincerely for your cause, that’s why you are always successful in doing what you try to do. Can you remember anything ever as hard as you could not do, which you really wanted to?” asked I.

“I will try to remember”, unsure Tavon said...I don’t get, why things happen that way...

As Tavon listened patiently I tried to explain more about life*... explaining his queries about uncertainties of life that could satisfy his intellect and strengthen his mind...“We should get best out of what we have as that is in our hands,” said I. “Be happy in what you get and your best effort would change it to the best...You will definitely get rewards for your hard work and I know you are going to be the best student of your class.”

---

*...Change is a law of Nature as it brings movement in life. - Behind this change is the “Supreme Power” –the Creator of life on earth, “Thyself God”. The force of His “Mystic

Initially confused Tavon looked relaxed and nodded his head in affirmation and smiled saying, "now I can understand so many things." Impressed and convinced Tavon said, "Thanks mom, for explaining all that to me, you're my best teacher."

"Cheer up! Cheer up!" I said, "You look so good in that happy mood".

Tavon's confidence restored and seemingly armed with assurance that better days lie ahead, he switched on music and started setting up room enthusiastically...

I enjoyed reading diary writes Jazara...I liked Laqueta's approach on life and how she convinced Tavon. Although I never believed in God, Laqueta's views left such a powerful impression on me...it really touched my conscious! ...I decided to take a break and closed the diary. As I got up to leave for my room, I noticed Tavon, who seemed to be very mature and studious.... I was happy for Elroy that he has a good friend in Tavon. Two of them had developed a very good rapport. Tavon was a senior and he cared and guided Elroy in his studies. ... I called Laqueta, "Hey Laqueta, are you busy?"

Not really, just helping Tavon. Have you finished reading?

Not all of it.

Energy" keeps working through principles of Nature propelling changes throughout the creation to maintain momentum of life such as movements of growth, renewal of life through birth and death, changing day and night and rotating seasons with ups and downs of temperatures ...Thus change is forced through the whole creation, whether it is the evolution of a species, or the interchange of various energy forms and physical matter,.

"Jazara, you can keep that diary with you and read all of it. I have already started the new one", said Laqueta.

Saying good bye to Tavon and Laqueta I left their room...

Change is movement; the unchangeable principle of Nature for the life to go on. The movement exists in every stage and form of life and creation whether it is a small cell in the body and its functional units working for cell to keep it alive or mega events happening around us in the nature, society and human beings world wide...

"But I only know that movement occurs in living beings, as I studied in Bio." Tavon said. ...

...That is a limited meaning as we study about visible body movements in the living beings. But my dear this is not only for living beings but it can be actually applied to the whole life and existence in nature...A phenomenon of constant change is taking place all over.

Creation at different levels with different magnitudes...We can experience this in change of objects, environment, and happenings in different societies. All the people are in movement constantly, not only because of their body movements but managing life and moving all through circumstances as a whole and the life goes on. The nonstop flow of thoughts effects change in consciousness of people that brings social change; changing habits, characters and behaviors of people...God has His design of things programmed for everyone, which we cannot know. ...

"Yes for the day, I never thought about life that deeply," I said to Laqueta, who was helping Tavon in his project. "I have also learned something today"...Jazara said to Laqueta.

A FAMILY

Laqueta writes...In no time we got settled down, at Elon's house and our life began anew as his family in Newtown. I started going to library for my job. It was an interesting job and I came across so many good books while I worked there, which I may have never seen otherwise. Schools were closed for the summer and the library used to be full of children. They were all over, on the computers, around bookshelves and C D racks, small kids read stories with parents in children's section and some kids used to huddle together in the conference room learning craft. This made the library very lively. Tavon also joined library as a volunteer for a few hours per week.

Living in new family at new place was exciting for Tavon. He enjoyed a lot, together with Jenny* and Jelly.* They went downtown, hanging out together, going for coffee to Starbucks, watching movies and shopping. They had a lot of fun at home, watching T.V., playing games and talking about stuff from movies and T.V. shows. Their favorites were The Simpson, Everybody Loves Raymond, Friends, etc............

Mealtime was a big time when everyone was around and children were chatting with each other about their activities of the day and we discussed with them any problems they had. They enjoyed eating variety of different non-vegetarian dishes cooked by Adara and vegetarian dishes cooked by me. Elon was happy as he shared same tastes, as did I and everyone enjoyed a healthy vegetarian change. I enjoyed cooking for first the time, together with Adara it was an interesting and an enjoyable experience.

---

*Laqueta's niece

As days passed by, Tavon got busy with his studies, as he was supposed to pass a test before joining his new class and he had to go through that course work on his own, without any tuition or help from any teacher. He started spending more time on studies, which reduced his time for family activities. I was happy he was so responsible about his work and I didn't have to worry about his studies. Soon, I joined another job, as income from one job was not enough to meet expenses and I too became very busy. Sometimes Adara complained that we are keeping to ourselves. She pointed out to Tavon to spend more time and go out with girls, not realizing that he had to prepare for test by himself, without any help. Perhaps Adara could not appreciate that Tavon's studies were his prime concern for which we came to U.S. Tavon always had independence in planning his days as and when he wanted to study, play, sleep or relax. We always gave him freedom of time and his own preference to choose his activities so that he can study in his best time of concentration. Even if we wanted, we could not spare more time for family than we were doing, to please Adara and the girls. Elon and Adara didn't seem to realize that I could hardly spare any time after my two jobs and all the work I did at home. Perhaps Adara's tolerance was short lived and signs of her intolerance started showing in her unpleasant behavior. Instead of appreciation for my efforts, Adara became spiteful and conjuring up contrived sarcastic comments. I ignored her diatribe to maintain congenial atmosphere. It was an unfortunate development but I kept up hope for a change in her behavior and maintained my patience.

I asked Tavon, "Is it possible for you to spend more time with Jenny and Jelly?"

Showing me his books, Tavon said, 'Mom, I have to read all these books. “If I keep hanging around with them when will I study?” “Mom”, he said again, “moreover Jenny says nasty things to me which I don’t like and that’s why I don’t feel like talking to her.”

I said, “You should try to ignore her as she is younger than you and still learning.”

“How many times can I ignore? I also want to talk back to her many times and could have already done it, had you not told to keep myself restrained. She deserves to be taught good lesson to put her words back in her own mouth,” Said Tavon.

I tried to appease him and appreciated his patience and tolerance and impressed upon Tavon to keep his cool.

He was still agitated and said, “Why should I tolerate Jenny, if she says anything wrong? You know how rude is she and I don’t want to be insulted all the time...“

“You are right, you should not tolerate anything wrong, “said I, sensing his feelings as he was right on his own right.

You know, “You are my darling son.” I said and assured him that he was perfectly right in deciding to not to tolerate anything that was wrong.

But my dear you need to understand that we cannot demand anything from them as we are under their obligation, while staying in their house. We can’t even say that Jenny is wrong. You know Adara’s attitude, she will not like us complaining against her and anyone of her family members and she will unnecessarily find a lame excuse for showing her attitude. Jenny may also rebel, if we complain and she can say more nasty things. You have seen how she yells at everybody, including her dad. Had her mom and dad realized this, they would have already rebuked her, anytime they found her misbehaving with us or anyone else. Adara neither cares about our requirements nor is she approachable and accommodating towards us so that our living could be more comfortable. She is so intolerant that she is always ready to comment on us on one pretext or other. Adjusting to this situation, ignoring their behaviors is only option. ...I hope Jenny will realize on her own, as she would grow ...

May be! But I have to deal with her, what she is right now. I cannot wait till she grows up to understand.

That's right; she will take time to learn on her own, until she grows up and becomes mature. Right now, only her parents can teach and pursue her for a better behavior. They never make the girls realize, that we are also a part of their own family and they need to respect us equally for our needs and sentiments as they expect for themselves...If Elon and Adara value us as family members they will themselves make room for an understanding and they can tell Jenny to control her behavior, as they are aware of everything happening in the house...Always remember, if your behavior is good, no one can hold you guilty and you will always feel good about yourself even if others don't appreciate. Your mind will reflect back your goodness and will not be guilty of any wrong doings.

Tavon understood the situation, but asked, "How can I control myself as I feel very bad when Jenny shouts at me? Jelly talks nicely to me and I like talking to her. Tavon reminded me of an incident which happened the other day during dinnertime. He said, "That is uncalled for how she keeps yelling at everybody, especially me".

Adara always ignored Jenny saying it's her teenage behavior without realizing that Tavon was only two years elder to her and still a young teenager but was a well behaved child. "I know," said I, "It is not easy to control oneself from such provocation, but try not to get into any arguments or pass comments on her so that she doesn't get any excuse to shout at you."

Tavon said, "Mom, don't you think it's good if I stay away from Jenny as I may also get angry on her."

I said, "O.K., that's better to stay away than getting into some altercations, and you should try to be good to everyone and behave nicely so that you are not at fault. You can talk to Jelly more as she is nice to you and avoid Jenny. Talk to Jenny whenever necessary but don't respond when you don't like her attitude or behavior. You know, I tolerate everything considering them to be my family members, thinking as if they are 'you'. I feel it's their nature and they don't understand as much as we do.

But Elon and Adara are as grown up as you and they should appreciate your work and your position as equal to theirs and they should make their children understand this.

"Yes, that's why I said, they don't understand and may be it's their nature; People's understanding can be different about the same thing as people evaluate things differently, mostly considering their self-interest only. Appreciation of human values and its realization does not come to all.

"When will they learn?" asked Tavon.

"I don't know! Don't worry about them; let's focus on our work. Forget about those things, as our work is most important and we should not let that suffer for any reason, I said." How considerate and caring should we be to one–another, is a self–learning that is realized with enlightenment of mind when your understanding grows...*

Listen Tavon, "Right now, we don't have any other options but to stay here and bear with everything, whether we like it or not, I think you can be more tolerant and increase your patience as you need to remember importance of your behavior to manage a peaceful environment that you need for your studies." To keep him in good morale, I said, "Everything will be okay, Just keep happy and do your work and be a good boy in the house so that no one complains about your behavior. That's it! I know you can do this." "Yes mom, I'll certainly do that and be assured that I will take care of my behavior. I will never give you a reason to worry about," said Tavon.

---

*...Actually, I thought this situation was very good in a way and Tavon would also become little more tolerant. This environment created compulsions for Tavon for doing things otherwise he may not have wanted to do. I felt this was God's plan for Tavon to learn a few things of life as he always got what he wanted. Because he was an obedient and responsible child, we always rewarded him with the freedom of making his own choices and decisions for himself. ...

BEHAVIOR DILEMMA

Laqueta continues...I didn't understand why Elon and Adara ignored to teach the girls to mix up with us and treat us like family. Instead of taking any positive action in persuading the girls, to behave well they sometimes played negative role too, through their behavior that diluted our efforts for creating bonds with them ...*

Yesterday, we were sitting in the T.V. room and Jelly was in playful mood; she jumped around sofa chairs and everybody tried to catch her. Elon was enjoying this very much as sometimes Jelly jumped into his lap and sometimes he caught her and hugged. Once I also tried to catch her ...

Elon shouted at me, "Don't you grab her."

Jelly immediately turned back, **running away from me. My arms were left open...

Hugs for Jelly were left behind,
In search of family ties...
My heart cried and mind turned blind!
That time, I wanted to ask Elon a question, about family line.

---

*...When Jenny and Jelly were small, they were just like other playful children and responded to me very well. Apparently, now they were grown up and no longer interested in cuddling or playing. Once grown up, children are individuals who have their own tastes, interests and hobbies. They make choices as per their limited, guided understanding until their own independent understanding of the life is build up...

** Elon's interference amounted to guiding Jelly to turn away from me...

Could you let Jelly understand, all people's hearts and minds?
How a child can learn equal rights?
We may not teach, wrong and right...
We should not misguide...
Give them freedom to decide...
A child's heart is kind,
A 'little mind' will always choose right...
I kept wondering about Elon's behavior and his mind...
Is he always ready to shout and fight?

Problems are not over when you have to live and deal with others all the time- -

Today evening, Tavon was miserable when I came back from work. He was in depression, crying uncontrollably. I tried to console him but to no avail. Turning on his favorite program, on T.V., I tried to distract him...Yet, I was struggling to get him out of depression, I heard Elon calling everyone for dinner. In vain, I tried to persuade Tavon to get back to normal and join everyone for dinner but he wasn't out of depression yet though he was much cooled down and composed. Reluctantly, leaving Tavon behind in upset mood, I went down to join everyone for dinner...

Adara asked, "Where is Tavon? Why hasn't he come down?"

I replied sadly, "He is crying as he is missing his Texas school and may not have dinner."

"That's O.K.", said Elon, "Why are you upset?"

Distraught and looking for some help I said, "He has been crying for the last two hours and his depression is not good for him and I am extremely worried for him."

To my dismay and shock, instead of any sympathy, Elon blurted out, shouting at top of his voice, "Go back to Texas," throwing his hands in air as his large eyes bulged out.

Keeping mum, I sat dumbfounded and appalled for a while! I wondered if I had said anything awful to anybody here that Elon shouted like that. I wanted to get up and go away as I was about to break down...Thank God! I managed to keep my control. Heartened, and bitterly swallowing my tears, I got up to drink water and joined back for dinner...After finishing dinner and washing the dishes, I went back upstairs.

Tavon was sitting quietly, lost in deep thoughts wiping his eyes. A concerned Tavon asked, "Are you O.K.?" Why did Elon shout so loudly?

Don't you worry; forget about that, he talks that way only.

But I heard, he shouted like a mad, "Go back to Texas". I got scared and thought he was angry at us. Does he want to send us back to Texas?

No! He is mad and doesn't know how to behave. You need not to be upset for anything I said. He knows well that it is not possible for us to move back there now.

Though I tried to pacify Tavon, Elon's behavior sent a chill through my nerves. The rude behavior of Elon uncovered his uncaring and unconcerned attitude that shook earth beneath my feet. The shallow bottom of weak support to which our emotions had been clinging until now became visible...Your family is where you are respected and cared for your needs equally. You get needed emotional support, uplifting you in hour you are down. Family support and sympathy is extended to share your problems to strengthen you when you are weak and sad. ...As the veil of hope and faith was lifted, there was hollow...nothing was there...what seemed to be support, sympathy and respect for our needs was gone!...Tavon had always felt at home until now but realized today that Elon was not his Dad but he was only Jenny and Jelly's daddy. He discovered harsh side of life and now knew expectations of sympathy or love from others could be transitory. ...We went out for walk around the block. A cold breeze outside was soothing and acted as tranquilizer, bringing Tavon back to his normal good mood. About half an hour after walk, Tavon started feeling hungry and we went back home for dinner. Tavon joined everyone in the T.V. room, after he had finished his dinner but I went back upstairs to our room to prepare for next day.

Each word spoken by Elon, especially "Go back to Texas" started hitting on my head, one after another, like serial blast explosions...I tried to relax and forget whatever happened. I picked up a book and started reading. After reading a few lines, I closed the book, as I could not concentrate. Elon's words were constantly hitting my mind. I was wondering how future days would be as this was just the beginning. If Elon is behaving this way, what could we expect from Adara? Elon was the person with whom we connected most as he had a direct relationship with us. He had committed to bear responsibility and take care of us, as we were his own brother's family. We trusted his words and moved in to stay with them. This person, whom we thought was most reliable, was a weak, unstable, unreliable and unpredictable person. He is not only insensitive and unsympathetic, but also so unconcerned for others afflictions... instead of any consolation or extending a helping hand, he does not hesitate to inflict more pain to persons who are already hurt. Would he react same way if any of his own family members, Adara, Jenny or Jelly were sad or upset, crying for even a couple of minutes?

Never...! He dare not do that...He can't say anything, even when someone is doing something wrong in his family as in case of Jenny.

"Go back to Texas!!" alerted my mind that started delving into whole situation...especially, Elon's harsh blast out. These were not just words uttered thoughtlessly without any sense or purpose by a small child or an insane person who is incapable to understand their meaning. It was a reflection of mind of that person who was highly qualified and knew all about situation and compulsions of our circumstances. I felt these words carried lots of information, which I should know...Why Elon behaved like this? Knowing our helpless situation, how could he utter those words? Elon's words "Go back to Texas" knocked on my mind constantly..., his behavior, flashed his attitude... It made me think about attitude and behavior of all family members and our equation of living with them...

How could he be so callous and say these words? He may have said so because he thought so! If he could think and say so, he could ask us to do that. Accordingly, he may ask us to leave his house the same way, as given how unconcerned he was, while he was saying, "Go back to Texas"...it could be another way of saying, 'go away'...

“Go back to Texas!!” in no time blew away peace of my mind and with that relations were lost, which were built over years on foundation of hopes, emotions, and faith...It burnt all ‘threads of relationships’, we were trying to build. My shattered mind kept thinking whatever it could...My mind in dilemma and confusion, tried to find answers to uncertainties lying ahead

A QUIET WAR

As I finished reading Jazara's email, Laqueta's life was as open to me as it was to Jazara. Jazara's fondness and concern were natural for Laqueta as both of them were together to share and care about each other's life at Newtown. I got up and cooked dinner quickly as it was my TV time.

A shoot out at a school, the news reader announced...

Dazed, I sat down,
As I listened to news headlines...
Wondered at the troubled times...
How is the volcano of violence...
Oozing out of little minds?
What...? Who guides them?
I tried to look behind the violent minds?
Why little minds are at war?
I want to find,
How a little heart becomes so unkind?
Where the violence strikes on their minds?

I switched off TV and sat down to pray for peace in minds and heal those who have suffered violence and crime. I took my pen and vowed to get back the peace to human life. I started probing violence and minds...Lost in minds, I didn't know where I was lying. I got connected with Laqueta's thoughts and with her mind...I went through war, where she did not fight. Elon's behavior played back, ...his language and actions in words... flashed through my mind...

I tried to sort out words, actions, thoughts and a violent mind...As

I searched into hearts and minds,...in no time, I became Laqueta and Tavon became mine...Every child like Tavon is now mine. Now Laqueta'a story is mine. I have to find peace for not only Laqueta and Jazara but for every other mind.

"Go back to Texas!!" Each letter in a word is like a miniscule particle, which may seem insignificant. But they become as powerful as 'bomb' when integrated together into word and phrase...uttered in volatile manner, they are loaded with ample potential energy, blowing up a person's composed mind in no time, leaving it restless, ruffled and troubled...

I got up and decided to spend some time on the computer. I started looking through news headlines...oops,...bombings and suicide bombings in Iraq and Afghanistan screamed through headlines. Everywhere, everyone seemed to be fighting wars...I turned off computer and got up to lie down to have some rest, to escape all wars and bombings, causing violence and crime...

"Go back to Texas!!" The 'explosion' was still rocking my mind, shattering my peace and hitting endless thoughts in restless psyche traveling through every past moment spent with Elon. I tried to clear my vision scanning all actions and behaviors. I heard Elon's language and tried to analyze words in that line..."Go back to Texas"...

I reasoned with my mind to ignore language of Elon's behavior and words of that line. Forget, it! That line doesn't mean anything! Elon didn't mean it. Then, why did Elon speak it? Did those words "Go back to Texas" had no meaning for Elon when he spoke them? If he doesn't mean it, why does he speak anything?

Does that mean, ...the words that we speak have no meaning?

Should words of a person's speech, do not matter in his behavior? Can language and speech, most important tools of human communication — be rendered meaningless and useless?

What did you say? ...Ha Ha Ha! Does that make any sense?

Human communication is based on meaningless and useless tools! It should not matter, what we write or speak! ...

Is that right? If that is right; then how do we communicate?

If words and speech do not matter, forget all about, language and try speaking without words! ...

How would we speak, without language and words?

That's funny! I don't get it, how? Hello, are you stupid? ... Think over...

Language is the most important ability of civilized human being. It is our means of communication that has accelerated development in every walk of life. Development of language makes us human beings. Civilization could grow only on platform of language and communication.

Every letter and word we speak is meaningful and valuable.Pick up any language and dictionary; No word is without any meaning. Every word originates in mind from thoughts, which are unspoken words lying dormant in consciousness until spoken out live.

Each word in that line, "Go back to Texas!!" too has a meaning.

Spoken words, 'specific sounds' are not mere sounds generated in some irrational manner; but each word is 'transmuted thought', that is, an individual's 'thought choice' waiting to be spoken as desired by person holding that 'word as thought' in his mind...for impressing upon others for desired actions, communicating one's thoughts through vocal behavior...

"Go back to Texas!!" "Go back to Texas!!"...

The explosions in my mind didn't stop! As if each word was a "latent bomb" and 'each letter' seemed exploding infinitely, ...unstoppable... How to stop? Where to stop? ...

News on computer had same stories...stories of bombings and suicide bombings causing havoc in the battlefield field created outside...bombs and wars cause destruction...Imagine, how tiny particles are packed with destructive power to form bombs. They could be Atomic and Nuclear bombs or some small crude bombs, capable of causing devastating destruction of property and killing people, holding potential threat of wiping out humanity and life on earth. These bombs engulf peace and people's life...so are these 'letter bombs' that suck peace out of mind...leaving wounded hearts and shattered minds...

War initiated by that line in 'my mind', has caused unprecedented damage and devastation, affecting my life. ...Any war destroys peace, love, trust and faith in people.

I wondered what if words and letters of this line "Go back

to Texas!" were made of chemicals; it would have destroyed everything around whole house with all its surroundings and inhabitants would have been lost in no time, Perhaps that has happened with these 'letter bombs' too, with only walls of house lying intact but a family is lost, destroying its ties, bonded through minds. Letters of this line too packed power that is no less than any chemical or bomb type...as they exploded like a bomb on my mind...

What is a family? What is a house? What is a home? I am seeking their meaning now, as I had never done before..."Go back to Texas!!" These words spoken by Elon were not silent letters printed on a paper. These were blasted live, causing fatal impact with destructive blow on my mind. These words were as powerful as live bomb and crashed 'world of hopes' and relationship ties, where members from two families mingled feelings and shared life...

It was quite late, sleep seemed to have disappeared in the blast's noise...Looking in the dark, I quietly waited for peace of night that always holds its calm, sharing it with all restless minds...slowly sliding them into sleep wrap...leaving all my worries to God, I didn't know, when I fell asleep with blessings divine.

---

*As Elon showed the way back to Texas, "...his shaky commitment surfaced through his thoughts, blowing questions on our survival" wrote Laqueta....it exposed the lack of sympathy, concern...there was no common ground left for the two families...and any importance of building ties of relationships vanished as their needs and circumstances had tied them together;...The blast caused through Elon's behavior language...shattered Laqueta and Tavon's minds, broke their tie of trust, faith...loss of all hopes separated them from Elon's family line and all the ties clinging to their hopes vanished in no time...The language and behavior of the people in the family make and break any ties...

A SEARCH FOR PEACE

Tring tring.........the alarm clock went off.... Oh, no!...I turned off the buzzer and slipped back into bed as usual and dosed off for some more sleep. Fortunately my phone rang up and woke me up again. I got up to get ready in time. Last night seemed to be long and tiring,...I wondered, why sleep didn't freshen up my mind? I felt tired as if I had walked miles...where did I go?...What was that? I tried to find...I scratched my head with comb umpteen times and tried to catch on all memories in my mind!...It was all in my dreams! My subconscious mind, probably worked on all problems, left with it last night...Anyhow I got up and started my day...

The morning was very busy and I concentrated on my work, forgetting all tensions. During break, I talked to one of my friends and dozed off for a couple of minutes to compensate for some loss of sleep from previous night. As day was over, I packed for home, brooding over evening chores and on the way I stopped for shopping at my daily store...

While walking back home..."Go back to Texas!!" became live with every step I tried to leave it behind. Why did it follow my mind? To know that, I have to follow it back, from blast of that line...I tried to pick up, what blast had left behind!...

"Go back to Texas!!"...
Letters and words of a line...
Shattered!... the calm and quiet mind.
The mind lost its sleep and missed its peace...
Aggression and fight in Behaviors, of people...

Only they can mind...
Circumstances, you can't hold...
Hold 'Thy Peace'...
And you don't whine!
You search it...
Thy Peace' you will find.

Living together is like, two objects, moving together, and that would make noise. Even while placing the two things together, they can cause noise, as it causes some friction. And friction between two things, moving together is law of nature. Noise can be minimized and it can be quiet, if you are careful and do not strike objects...that will keep noise in careful stride...

How to manage the human with noise?
What to do when they are not in 'Peace' line?
How can 'Peace' be mine?
While I was lost in that line...
Thought after thought came!
How that 'Peace', will I find?
As the wind blew softly...
The bells, outside the window...
Chimed and chimed...
Then there was quiet, quiet and quiet...
Quiet 'Peace', welcomed by the night...
The sleep held the 'Peace'...
And quiet became the chime!
After a long night of sleep, plentiful of peace...
I woke up to the music of the chime...
It's each tinkle rhymed...

It's peace and peace time...
Its peace and peace time...
Its peace and peace time...
The mind in delight, heard the tinkle of chime...
I bowed my head to the 'Divine'
And thanked for the peace times.

I gazed at my face, through mirror covered with haze... As I cleaned haze; room was lit up with a glare, as if peace shined through a night mare...Ah! Said my conscious, it's so precious... As I untangled my hair, my mind declared...

I want to hold, the feast of peace...
Which is everyone's treat!
I determined to see 'Peace' for no one's, cease...
Well, I have to achieve this feast...
Where, all souls and minds can rest with peace.

As I cleaned my comb, weaned away thoughts of blasts and bombs... tinkle bells chimed again and with a tinkle each time, a thought crossed my mind...I remembered Gandhi, messenger of Peace! I started remembering his teachings, especially nonviolence he practiced and preached. He asked to follow path of peace and brave violence with tolerance..., his famous quote, "If someone slaps on your one cheek offer him another cheek too...

...I heard meow, meow...a cat outside was crying like a child...child of my heart, told my mind, it is not right...my thought hit my conscious...

What? My conscious seemed to have reservation and resistance to any action and behavior where violence is high.

Ah! A thought warned my mind, how could a child take violence in his stride, if someone gave on his face a slap, tight...This is how, devils are born, making violence their might, intimidating a kind human with terror and violent fight...

The doubt knocked my mind and it started to vacillate about this advice, accepting any violence for peace doesn't seem right....a small child, cannot bear torture of devils, unkind people...we need to broaden our understanding and devise a way, that goes through the mind and makes people kind...

I wished there were some easy ways, which children find interesting, and entice to follow them. It is really difficult and confusing! I don't understand...what to do? ...My scientific mind started searching further and was curious, how to find a simple formula, an equation, which is easy to understand and acceptable, especially to the young with inquisitive minds ... and those minds, high on aggression and suffer for lack of 'Peace' in their lives ...and violence or frustration make them blind.... Violence is bursting into their behaviors and minds, bouncing them down to depression or throw them out of balance all the time.

That will be tomorrow's human kind! Do we want such a mankind? Every child is divine, and the Divine loves every life. They do not want aggression and violence. It is only the Devil's ploy which has to be foiled.

Save the little angels
From the violent tangles
They trap in the devil's scheme
Of failing peace...
Provoking people with aggression
Handing violence to the beasts
Who lead the crime and violence in the street ...
Angels can defeat the violent beasts
Cool your minds with peace, the aggression will cease...
The anger will retreat; keep your mind at ease
That will win you peace
Devils and Beasts will get defeat...
In their 'violence-scheme' and minds filled of greed.

A formula that is easily understandable! ...Think over...How most volatile elements of physical matter lay together inert until they were made to react... Today all Chemistry, Physics or any other science of matter seemed to be more important to me - searching for human equation of peace... simple and easy guideline to create 'Peace'...

Peace equation – peace formula for human interactions! – It may be just like a physical equation or chemical equation in Physics or Chemistry. A formula of human chemistry and physics! ...May be a formula to alter chemicals of human mind and to control physical actions of human behavior?

I think, violence also needs to be understood...

Violence is only an action
It takes a shade from interaction

With the human mind and its own habit of virtue or vice.
It can be war inside the mind,
May be an action of human crime,
And doling out a war and terror in these times.

My mind pondered over an idea and thought of working towards Peace Formula, which could help to build an understanding about peace and show the way to cultivate peace as I find every other individual in trouble, looking for some peace. Growing social violence and increased aggression are not only matters of concern in adult people but frequent violent behaviors in children too are a matter of grave concern.

An individual evolves only in the light of understanding, which plays a key role in human behavior. Understanding makes the mind learn about one's own self and others, showing the truth of life. Healthy human interaction can only be built on an understanding of caring and sharing life. A person's thoughts and conscious, along with his emotions and the factors around an individual must influence any behavioral action that results into violent or non-violent actions, through interaction with one's environment and people.

Violence does not arise on its own...
'Ill will' it does not hold...
It goes with the human mind...
The hand that holds all the action of will and resolve...

The riddle of violence and peace...
Each one of us can solve.
Peace is on hold...
Till your mind's 'choice of peace' is bold.

It has to be our will's goal.
Hold the will of violence,
And let Peace unfold.
Strengthen your will...
And make the peace bold.

THE PEACE FORMULA

Peace is the soul of creation. It keeps whole universe balanced, taking into its stride all extremes of natural changes and upheavals of human action. Violent behavior of man and his cruel exploitation of creatures and natural environment are responsible for plight of humanity, where hunger, disease and natural disasters, stare at the face of mankind's civilized future. An order of balance has to be maintained throughout creation, balancing systems and maintaining harmony and stability of life on earth. We, all are responsible to hold this balance together. None other than human beings tampers with this peaceful balance. Loss of balance results in natural calamities and environmental degradation, where disease brings misery and pain to man, who ultimately loses his peace due to his misdeeds.

Human being, in the pursuit of becoming 'master of universe' has wreaked havoc on earth. Violence unleashed by him has brought misery to life and destruction of nature and the peaceful balance of the world has been pushed to brink of collapse. In a polluted and unhealthy environment, violence is blowing up people's minds and war is looming large on the horizon along with rise in Nature's fury. Not one, but many are trying to be masters, forgetting the one and the only master – creator of the universe – Omnipresent, Supreme Power...we know as mysterious God.

Modern extravagant life styles are increasingly fascinating people and to seek it, they are chasing money, lured by its power to purchase dream material life. It has created a continuous struggle in people's minds; especially youngsters are lured into this rat race to become the winners at all costs. Young minds, without comprehending their own strengths and overlooking other avenues of life are lured into blind run, unaware of pitfalls and cracks of downfalls in this steep path... They tread aggressively as superheroes on a battlefield, for a fight to reach that glittered street, which is a temporary glow with deceiving tweets. That flight and fight, results into stress and disease, with their bodies starving for rest and peace. This war ends in self -defeat, as war is unable to provide a happy balance of life, which is a feat of peace..., bestowing health and harmony in a happy treat...

Superheroes of action-filled stories are always projected as winners, who enact violence through their action. These glorified heroes thrill little minds and train them for violence obscurely, packaged as entertainment and glory. TV and the Internet are flooded with such programmed heroes sold through movies, games, etc. This conditions little minds to become superheroes, with a glorified victory of violence and turns them into aggressive minds. These virtual heroes with glamorous images have captured the thinking, and consequent actions of children, leading to violent behaviors, crime and antisocial activities...

Catastrophic headlines about every violent story add to the confusion of young minds, prompting them to enact violence in another violent story, just to flash their super actions, to get recognition and glory through daunting headlines...These heroes and their super actions inspire youngsters with 'do it yourself' messages... No wonder, a terrorist might be one of today's superheroes, trying to impress others by their aggressive super actions. They are further misguided by terror mongers and crime wheelers, sent by devils to human paradise...

Creators of these violent, virtual superheroes have relegated real life heroes like Mahatma Gandhi to the oblivion. War of violent superheroes has overshadowed superpower of 'Peace,' undermining peaceful super-minds, people who have stayed on the path of non-violence that led to glorious victories have become history of past... A real super hero, in real human story is a challenge, in these violent times...

Heroes take up challenges. Winning 'Peace' through Peace is the biggest challenge. Winning over powerful armies without any warfare is super - super heroic action! Peace is life's super- fine action, of a mind, which is kind and sides with nonviolence, caring for others lives. Anyone can take up this challenge and achieve Peace! Be winning superhero! Anyone, who can arise peace is a winner, in real human stories of these times of violence and crime.

Violence, all around world is not only rising day-by-day but fears of world war loom large to engulf humanity. Extremism is on rise, making life hell for people. Peaceful living is becoming a dream in this chaotic era of escalated crime and terror all around. Non-violence seems defeated, seeing violence flare up, in every other mind, ...

Violent Heroes are fighting, violence, violently, to end violence!!

Peace is obscured in minds as violence is dominating human life. Non-violence seems impossible, as there seems no end to violence, which has corrupted many people's minds and corruption is preying on people's rights, disdaining peace from conscious and people's minds...

Violence fought by violence is multiplying violence...an end to violence is not visible...violence can crush each life as violence is an action of destruction and can become dead end of action of human or his life...

Can there be peace in my sight?
May I not lose hope by the time?
Can I keep hope alive till the peace comes to my sight?

Peace is a twinkling light,
It's seen by a kind eye...
With the rays of hope,
It shines and twines.
Hey! Hope holds the Peace high...
It twinkles and always shines...
Just hold the hand of hope high,
Violence and fight is not right'
They will fail to stand by the 'peace might'
Delight in twinkle of the 'peace light'...
Peace brings tranquility to the mind...
Let the peace shine and arise through every mind.

Hey, is that a dream of previous night?
Can the way to peace be in my sight?
Will the people end violence and fight?
Will they learn that violence is a wrong choice?
Will the peace rise to glorious heights?
Will the peace be every mind's delight?

...The questions bubbled through my mind, ...It searched and searched... there...my conscious replied...

Peace is a winner, it will twinkle and shine...The path of non-violence will be fine.

Weak is 'wine of peace'... twined with violence, ... violently growing aggressive minds like weeds... non-violence always dives in 'violent strikes'... worried is my mind for...

People's will for a violent thrill...
It has killed the will for a non-violent drill.
How will non-violence win and peace arise?
Poltergeist of violence
Creates fear all the time,
Afraid I am
Way to the peace I cannot find
This monster of violence reigns
Every street and the wicked mind
Where is the way to peace?
I cannot find...

Hey! Take up challenge, and be a super hero! There is always a way. There is a way to peace too. Way to stop violence! We can together create way of our own choice...

...Show me the way?

'Peace' is way to 'Peace'!! (As Gandhi ji said," There is no way to peace; peace is way." Peace is not an end but it is a means.)
What are ways or means of 'Peace'?

Be Peace! ***Support Peace!*** ***Give Peace!***
Think Peace! ***Keep Peace!***

How can one even imagine peace with so much of unrest and violence around? I don't understand...

O.K.! Calm down and relax! *...Let's commence on 'Peace'...*
Be quiet and silent! ...
When your aggression drives you to anger or fight, ...
Come back to your mind!
Let it make peace, a choice...
Once you decide now, always make peace your choice!
Tell this to your mind forever...
It will remind the quiet and peace at every step in your life...
*And peace will always be your might. ...**Right!*** ...This is my way to find peace...Keep walking on this path – you will find 'peace light'...

Peace lights up, all the ways in mind,
That is how the peace can be your guide...
Lighting peace in your life...
It guides and glides you through the life.
Send thoughts of peace to your mind,
You have to act on thoughts of peaceful life,
Peace creates peaceful actions,
Sliding away aggression,
Arise and rise peace, when anger tries to rise.
Anger, aggression and violence will lag behind...
Always keep holding peace high and high.

Here is a simple formula to understand Peace. It's a peace formula for creating Peace. It can be your 'Peace formula' too. It is a formula to enlighten and achieve Peace for one and all. Practice and make it your way of peace, PLEASE.

This formula can be described to and adopted by all for a way of peace to every life -

THE PEACE FORMULA

It is an empirical equation of peace values that can be helpful in understanding and creating peace.

PEACE = (BEHAVIOR + INTERACTION) (VIR^N - VIC^N)

Where-

Behavior = Ic + Thought + Action + Ch + U factor
+ Mind + Emotions

Interaction = C + Environment + Conflict
+ Action (verbal + physical)

VIR^N = number of Virtues

VIC^N = number of vices

Ic = individual conscious

C = collective conscious

Ch = choice

U = understanding (Wisdom, Needs, Society, Age, Gender, Language, Will, and Health etc. are various factors that affect an individual understanding)

This is a winner's formula! It guarantees Peace. Each human being needs and wants peace. It is an equation for achieving individual peace as well as collective human peace. We need to work on values of peace and cultivate values that create peace.

This is a simple and concise formula for a general understanding of peace. A detailed description of constituents of the Peace formula will explain their inclusion in formula. Understanding of these constituents is important they bear direct impact on our behavior and cultivation of peace. Understanding of peace values purifies our conscious and strengthens our mind that has to decide right action and right choice to arise peace, making peace a choice...

Definition of Peace

"When you see the Earth for what it is, you couldn't see any borders. You couldn't see any signs of wars... It was just pure peace and beauty... You wonder, 'How could people ever do things to harm it?"– Anousheh Ansari, a space tourist, on seeing the earth from afar

Peace comes along with us from beginning of our life but this material world starts war on our mind. A desire stimulates, sending signals to mind, with want of material and an emotional need. It interacts with body and conscious guides, thoughts carry massage of conscious to mind that begins action of life. A search begins by human being as his mind reacts; he acts his karma on his way to life..., He cannot decide as he is confused to find another human, ...struggle in life arise... 'Peace' is challenged by 'War' in struggle of life.

Mind didn't know the war until another human was unkind. As the struggle began, war followed life and human lost his peace of mind...

Each mind has to define,
It's own peace and balance in life.
Peace is blessed to every mind with its life.
Each mind has to light it,
To illuminate its way to life,
Arise and rise peace from a twinkle that shines in your mind,
That peace will grow to sunshine
It will always stay with you,
Be a human kind,
Rise peace it will delight your heart and light your mind.

Peace is the first essential element of creation that constitutes life. It is latent divine energy inherent in every life on planet. It is universal life connection, core power centre of stability. It is eternal power that makes all action of our life possible and balances nature allowing action of all other forces playing through cosmos.

Perhaps it is divine power of Creator, who controls nature and natural balance of life through this variable power of life. Peace can, therefore, be described in various ways.

Peace is source of contentment due to its divine connection. All of us connect together through conscious of peace. Peace power gives us strength and courage to be kind and loving. Peace gives freedom of thought and action in boundless space and time, in each individual mind. Longing for peace is a natural desire of all living beings as it brings back balance of mind with its required pause of rest and relaxation after an action. It has to be the responsibility of all of us, to make it possible to retain harmony and joy in all spheres of life, by making peace a choice.

Law of peace is law of nature that is unchangeable. Each individual's conscious records his actions and he loses peace from his life if he fails to maintain balance of his mind, respecting every life. Since peace is divine it entails equal love and freedom to all living beings and stands behind justice, to support right of each individual life.

Disruption of peace is a crime against nature, life and creation, a sin that is unpardonable, for which we have to undergo punishment in one or the other way, at a destined stage. To preserve peace is preserving human species as well as preserving creation.

Peace is ultimate power and force of life that makes life happy, at all times. It helps our mind in struggle of life, brings back its balance and harmony from time to time...It gives time and space to mind, creating clarity of thought and understanding to make a right choice in journey of life. Give way to peace to arise in mind...

Reviewing Augustine's definition of peace (Friendship and society: an introduction to Augustine's practical philosophy - By Donald X. Burt), Augustine talks about the need to maintain an 'ordered balance' in a person's body and physical life at all levels of his interaction with his existence. "...Beginning of peace for individual comes when love is well-ordered and objects of such love are possessed. For a person to have perfect peace there must be internal and external harmony. The body must have an ordered balance among its parts: the soul, an ordered satisfaction of its appetites. Sensitive appetites must seek neither too much nor too little of those material things necessary for sustaining physical life. Intellectual appetites must reflect correspondence between desire and moral values. A person's internal peace depends on good order between body and soul and health in living a wholesome life."

Peace begins within an individual and it spreads to whole world through his conscious and soul.... A human being, like other organisms, is an integral part of nature and its interaction with all entities of nature requires an ordered balance at all levels, including his body, mind and soul. For maintaining an order in every arena of his life, in his relationships of interactions with other objects, he has to maintain balance in his own body and actions first. For maintaining external harmony, it is essential that our body retains internal harmony and a balance of mind. These external and internal harmonies together create Peace. Internal harmony in our body requires healthy balance of actions at all levels, spiritual, mental and physical. A person who possesses internal harmony reflects it in his character and behavior, exhibits peace through his actions that are conducive to external harmony. A harmonious interaction with others as well as peaceful actions, such as habits and behavior maintain an ordered balance and peace in one's environment.

Components of peace

Components of peace are attributes of human character and life that may break or create peace in every individual and his life. Peace is cumulated as collective peace, together by people through creating external harmony in their social life, creating an environment of peace, throughout universal life

Life is momentum,
Neither it's a story of war nor peace,

It is a human being,
Who creates war or peace!
Confused is he,
Peace, he cannot see...
He fails to decide,
What should be the right choice?
War or peace!
War is the end...
Peace is the symbol of life,
Confusion should not fail us to decide,
Peace is the right choice.

Human history tells only about wars and their heroes who destroy peace. We memorize wars, as we don't know history of peace. Perhaps life has been lived around wars and violence that did not let us see peace. When there is no war, only then we can say there is peace. The only time of peace we know is 'no war' time.

War or peace! Each makes any sense only with the human being. If we keep diving into history and dead human beings, we will fail again and again to see peace. But peace lives life after life as our conscious can see...it resides with a human live...

The story of life goes,
With the human, live...
Peace comes along with soul,
Life begins with action in the mind...
Where, pleasure or pain arise,
Conscious creates thoughts,
Thoughts are mind's guides,
Mind guides body

Interact-mind, thoughts and body...
Play through behaviors,
And some thoughts initiate...
Struggle in the body,
And conflict in the mind.
The human either begins...
War on his life...
Or creates Peace to his delight!
Our hearts and our minds,
Play with the pleasure and pains of life.

An individual's interaction with his environment initiates action in his body and mind..., stirring his conscious, thoughts and emotions that interact with body through brain, initiating electrical impulses in nerves, bringing a chemical change inside body of an individual that directs action of body outside, called behavior that is language and action of mind...

Since peace depends on an individual and his actions and interaction with his social environment, understanding of following components of peace is essential: - Conscious, Thoughts, Mind, Emotions, Virtues, Vices, Action, Choice, etc.

Thought phenomenon and Conscious

Perhaps conscious is inherited as subconscious that remains in unconscious state. It has been evolving through numerous lives since evolution of life on earth. It is inherited through generations, conditioned with thoughts of observation and experience, acquiring a thought pool where each thought becomes an individual's own thought. Mind and brain interact after conscious directs required thought that initiates action in mind.

Thought is the sole phenomenon that ensures flow of infinite life movement, keeping creation alive constantly – forever. Life forms may change but thought does not die. The thought pool develops conscious through exchange of thoughts and evolves through various lives with varied environments and perceptions imbibing the wisdom of observation and experience through generations retaining thought information as genetic code, transferred through inheritance.

URL: http://www.hyponoesis.org/ describes -"What is the process of thought? Thought is, in essence, the active response of memory in every phase of life. We include in thought the intellectual, emotional, sensuous, muscular and physiological responses of memory. These are all aspects of one indissoluble process. All these are one process of response of memory to each actual situation, which response in turn leads to further contribution to memory, thus conditioning the next thought."

"...Thought itself is in an actual process of movement. That is to say, one can feel a sense of flow in the 'stream of conscious' not dissimilar to the sense of flow in movement of matter in general. May not thought itself thus is part of reality as a whole)(David Bohm: Wholeness and the Implicate Order, 1992)" (p. ix)

Life action goes on, through interaction of thoughts. Thought creates impressions and perception that make us aware of existence of life, environment and other physical and biological attributes constituting creation...

Creation has so many mysteries beyond human understanding. The mysterious actions of nature must have a definite system of control. Maybe a parallel, invisible world is operating through subtle actions, such as phenomenon of thought – conscious that is beyond human perception.

Forces of disintegration, degeneration and death are continuously operating in nature, as are forces of creation and cohesion - peace and love, rejuvenating powers maintaining balance of life.

Swami Sivananda has described thought and its power in his book "THOUGHT POWER" as "Thought is the greatest force on earth....Everyone has his own thought-world....You can move the world through thought-force. Thought has great power. It can be transmitted from one man to another man. The powerful thoughts of great sages and Rishis of yore are still recorded in the Akasa (Akasic records). ...

Thought moves with tremendous velocity. Those who entertain sublime and pious thoughts help others, who are in their vicinity and at a distance also. ...A pure thought is sharper than edge of a razor. Entertain always pure, sublime thoughts. Thought-culture is an exact science.

Every thought, irrespective of its origin translates into action affecting the balance of life in this universe – similar to votes required to tilt the balance of victory. Our thoughts and actions might not always seem to affect us directly therefore we underestimate its impact.

Those who harbor thoughts of hatred, jealousy, revenge and malice are very dangerous people. They cause unrest and ill will amongst men.

Every thought that you send out is a vibration, which never perishes. It goes on vibrating every particle of the universe and if your thoughts are noble, holy and forceful, they set in vibration, every sympathetic mind.

Unconsciously all people who are like you take thought you have projected and in accordance with capacity that they have, they send out similar thoughts. The result is that, without knowing the consequences of your own work, you will be setting in motion great forces which will work together and put down lowly and vicious thoughts generated by the selfish and wicked."

Enriching your conscious with thoughts of peace will create peace around you, along with your mind that will show in developing a person's peaceful behavior. That way, we can train our minds to make the choice of peace by entertaining thoughts of peace and rejecting thoughts of anger, violence, war, injustice, crime and other negative and antisocial thoughts. Holding ill will towards others, hurts the collective conscious and causes social disharmony.

To know and practice peace, we have to understand the conscious and mind. Each individual inherits a conscious that guides his mind for action throughout life; it saves all thoughts and interacts with new thoughts. A constant communication between collective conscious and individual conscious takes place, through the network of thoughts to maintain harmony in life. Various thoughts carrying messages of information keep bubbling through collective conscious. Each mind has freedom of thought choice that gives us ideas about life. Now each thought is our idea saved in our conscious and it acts in our mind. As a person's mind takes a decision, the body follows the mind. Behavior, habits and actions, which we can observe are actions, played together by body and mind with individual conscious as their guide.

A cooperation of body and coordination of its actions with the mind, when it retains harmony of action and an ordered balance in behavior, it establishes peace in conscious that stabilizes the mind. A balance of action is not always sustained as our conscious is under constant change. Contradiction and conflict are playing through circumstances, as collective conscious has to guide each individual conscious to keep moving with harmony of nature and life.

Our conscious is a mystery,
We need to understand.
It varies from stage to stage,
Has a different story from face to face.
Mind is confused...
It changes from age to age.
It keeps evolving, higher and pure
One thing is for sure,
Body plays, life's role,
Conscious may create, life's stage,
With mind, it plays a game.
Conscious, we may or we may not understand!
Together, we play creator's game!

Thought interaction between the conscious of two individuals creates conflict, which they do not understand. This conscious game of conflict and concord remains a mystery, only the conscious can understand, which directs different individuals on different paths...

Contradiction ingrained in duality,
In nature and life's centre stage!
Where conflict of the thoughts in mind,
Moves life on two sides, the peace or war times!
One says its night,
The other says its day!
Two minds are in confusion,
Conflict has its way.
One is through
Peace.
The other way can stray into,
Violence,
When, it is not resolved in a peaceful way.

To unfold the mysteries and complexities of life, the mind has to pass the test of conflict and solve it in a peaceful way...Otherwise humanity will perish in violence and time will not let life survive if peace does not prevail....

Since the conscious of individuals establishes communication through direct or indirect interaction with each other, it is important to first understand one's own conscious and thoughts that affect one's own behavior. That will affect the behavior of the other individuals; ...It is like a two way street where thoughts exchange information. The individual conscious of people with varied understanding of the mind plays through emotions and behaviors..., leaves their impact on thoughts, building collective conscious of their time and in turn affect the social environment of every life.

Virtues and vices,
Two shades of life,
Get mixed in human social life.
Virtues are like the daylight,
That shines through the individual,
And strengthen his might.
Vices are dark of the night,
Vanish in the virtue's bright light.
Vices trick your emotions,
And blind your mind,
So you cannot see the truth of life.
Virtues integrate humanity,
Vices get humans lost in...
Hate, lust, greed, malice...
Anger, violence and crime...
Injustice and behavior unkind,
We should not compromise virtues...
It's the time for all to decide...
Get out of the dark of vices,
See the virtuous light,
Purify the conscious and the mind,
With the thoughts, virtuous and kind,
Vigor of virtues upholds,
Equal freedom and justice,
Creating harmony and joy in people's life.

As we are suffering in social violence and crime, each of us has to introspect our own mind, why vices are on rise and virtues are hard to find. Society and social institutions project a collective conscious, which has been created together by the conscious of individuals, creating social systems, groups, cultures, states and nations...Social evils are the result of loss of virtues, as vices have overpowered people and social institutions have been degraded with corruption, injustice and unequal distribution of money, materials and jobs, subjecting people to discrimination, exploitation, deprivation, oppression, bias and prejudice that has thrown people into hard times. The lives of all people are affected, making people resort to anger, rebellion and violence, creating unrest in the collective conscious.

Virtues and vices are inherent in the conscious of all human beings and our minds are free to make their own choices on the path of life. Virtues are the strength of human mind that gives pleasure to pass the test of time. They shine through individual character and behavior, which can conquer the mind's will. Virtues nourish the soul and keep the mind noble and kind.

Vices start rising in the human child as he grows and explores his life. His conscious perceives that virtues are compromised and vices are practiced with delight, while he is still naïve. The little mind starts learning vices on his way to life, who doesn't know, what is wrong and what is right. Blame should go to people with evil minds, who are responsible for the rise of vices, due to the decline of virtues.

Once grown up, the individual tries to take control of his life and is free to decide and makes his own choice, out of virtue and vice, that would be his will and action of mind. This choice will make a difference to his life, as it will affect his actions and peace of mind, while the conscious records all that action and reminds, our mind. The freedom in life brings balance to your mind that has the power to decide and analyse your own thoughts and life, maintaining your control and balance of mind.

Virtues are bold and strong, shine like sunlight; they are human pride and they don't need to hide. Vices can dump you any time in the struggle of life. They grow so fast and high, you will lose your mental balance as others take control of your life. You can ride vices as long as they can be hidden from others sight. You cannot deceive your own mind as your vices and virtues are recorded in your conscious and flashed back to your mind.

Emotion is the 'motion',
Can drive you through...
Promotion or demotion...
With conscious and the mind...
It moves through your body and brain...
It plays your life's game...
To keep life on rails,
It takes control of brain,
Watch out this 'E- motion'
That drives your thoughts,
And thoughts your behavior,
Your life may derail,
When, the control of 'E-motion' fails.

Emotions are the feelings, which influence an individuals behavior through physiological changes in the body, brain and the mind's thought process. Thoughts are carriers of emotions, linked to the mind and conscious. Some basic emotions must exist in our subconscious that plays through our instincts and reflexes. Thought communication with another conscious generates corresponding emotions during interaction with other individuals.

Emotions play a major role in our behavior as they affect our thought pattern and our body's sensory system. Various factors, such as gender, age, family, religion, culture and nation, influence our emotions and they play differently under influence of these factors. Therefore it is important to broaden our understanding and exercise control over our emotions to manage balanced behavior. Our conscious inherits and retains our emotional experiences in subconscious memory, which affect our mind as well as our body's health.

A common occurrence of state of emotional shock in people can be seen, that may result in heart attack or failure to breathe in an emotional reaction to a situation of fear or news of the death of a loved one. Almost all chronic diseases, such as asthma, arthritis, skin problems, blood pressure, thyroid and other hormonal disturbances such as women's diseases are a few examples of diseases arising from emotional disbalance, which influence the systemic functioning of the endocrine glands in our body. The body's organs fail to carry out their normal healthy functioning under emotional distress or excitement and to counter emotional stress, the body produces toxins that result in various diseases. Therefore, understanding emotions and learning to control them is very important for emotional detoxification that helps in building health.

Emotions can also be called the conscious' body intelligence that works through instinct and reflexes. Emotional intelligence controls body actions through the endocrine and nervous systems. The sense of touch and movement (somatic-sensory sensations), which is the most important emotional pleasure of a human being, enriches his mind with pleasure and self assurance of his life that creates a will in mind to live on. A close body interaction between two human beings provides a touch of comfort and satisfaction of the existence of a common bond between the two: Just as a small child feels comfortable, secure and satisfied in his mother's lap, which he trusts and knows, where he belongs, through touch and vibrations of body movements.

It is perhaps that spiritual connection which drives us towards each other and connects us all. When we disconnect from spirit, lost in the material world, our spiritual health declines and we become selfish and egotistical. We drift away from each other as we lose the spiritual connection and live in pride and hatred, becoming unkind to other human beings and keep on searching for lifes truth lost in pleasure and pains of a worldly life.

Virtue and Vice write peace in life!

All emotions are created naturally to enable action on the way of our life. Each conscious has ingrained emotions and virtue or vice, is a prompt for mind to enable action, at all times, on way to destiny of life. Virtues and vices are part of most complex emotional process that involves conscious, mind, thoughts, brain, heart, body and innumerable variables that include various individual factors (desire, will, belief, needs, goals, impressions, perceptions, age and gender etc.) and environmental factors (family, relationships, caste, friends, community, culture, religion and nation etc.) involved in individual interaction, while an individual lives his life.

Since we started living in society, our individual lives did not remain independent. Interdependence on each other takes control of living out of our hands and does not let us always have our choice. Every emotion is virtue if it allows for harmony in your life with the peace of your mind. Innumerable factors fused into an emotion and the related action cannot be assessed and no human can be eligible to define line of separation between virtues and vice for others life. Each one of us has to identify our own line of demarcation between virtues and vice as each individual is his own witness and it is a matter of his own mind. While we decide that line, we have to remember that the purpose of life can only be served through living this life. Struggling between virtue and vice, these emotions keep swinging, until your mind draws line between two that is how your mind decides action in your life.

Attachment of our desires, to particular beliefs, create positive thoughts for objects we value and want to possess and negative thoughts we want to avoid because our mind has fears and dislikes, which becomes our act of will through creation of corresponding thoughts. But this value judgment attached to objects might be judged differently by other person, as it is based on general belief of good and bad value attributed to objects and their values. Every individual should develop own understanding about what is good or bad for him, as values change with situation and relationships of social groups and organizations etc. But value of humanity is unchangeable and if you are kind hearted, you will never fail to side with virtues and your mind will always climb up the virtuous ladder every time...

A virtue or vice is the particular trait of that state of human character that originates as a thought and develops as a secondary emotion in body that effects action of mind and behavior in an individual. The importance of virtues and vices lay in their moral values that are helpful to an individual in interactions with people and making a choice of thoughts to make decisions for life and living. There are primary feelings, the first emotions, felt at first reaction of mind and its thought interaction. Virtues and vices are secondary emotions created in response to primary emotions, by thought interaction between individual conscious and mind.

A thought with an idea,
Becomes a virtue or vice,
Your mind has to analyze...
The conscious may not define,
Your mind has to decide,
It has to interact with the brain,
That has to run the body train,
The idea is now your 'brainchild'
It's in your hands and mind...
How you feed your 'brainchild'?
If you feed it with the thoughts 'evil',
It will grow fast into a 'devil'.
Your 'brain child' will glow and shine,
With the virtuous thoughts in your mind,
The glow and shine of the virtuous light,
Will illuminate your life's path,
Your 'brainchild' will get smart,
It will be humble and kind,
With the virtuous thought diet,
Delight of virtuous life will be your might,
The virtuous light is divine,
It will illuminate your spirit in this life.

The virtues are "morally valuable" character traits, accepted universal human values conducive to well-being of all. They are upright, good intentions of people who want to do and act good and right, driven by will of mind to do good and right. To develop our spiritual health and evolve our conscious we must educate ourselves with knowledge of basic moral principles. Human beings are gifted with freedom of will, logic and reasoning to make a choice of action to maintain harmony in life. Moral virtues are natural guides for strengthening mind, they help us to perfect our natural faculties (intellect, will, feelings and emotions, etc.), achieving optimum functioning of mind and brain.

We should practice virtues because every good act has good effect on humanity. Virtues promote integrity of individual character; strengthen peace, justice, freedom, equal rights creating harmony in society. True virtues are nature of spirit and they arise in human beings from spiritual motivation. Perfect harmony in body and mind, which can connect with the soul through spiritual high is supreme human state. Our conscious always tries to achieve that perfect harmony through our thoughts and actions.

Thoughts with gist and intention of producing naturally good actions, from natural motivation of individual's spirit create harmony and spiritual rise in an individual. They are useful not only to virtuous individual but for health and well – being of all life. These are desirable features and admirable qualities that strengthen mind, creating health and peace. Such pure thoughts and actions produce positive and healthy vibrations that radiate positive influence all around creating goodness and well being. Virtuous thoughts should become 'habit of mind' that builds not only healthy body and sound mind but also improves spiritual health, creating healthy and harmonious social environment, through peaceful behavior.

Peaceful individual's conscious strengthens peace in other people's life through collective conscious. Peace is power of virtues and they can write peace for every life.

Why wise favor virtues over vice?

"We make a ladder for ourselves of our vices, if we trample those same vices underfoot.

Saint Augustine

"Man's natural character is to imitate; that of the sensitive man is to resemble as closely as possible the person whom he loves. It is only by imitating the vices of others that I have earned my misfortunes."

Marquis de Sade

"No company is preferable to bad. We are more apt to catch the vices of others than virtues, as disease is far more contagious than health."

Charles Caleb Colton

We should practice virtues as they do well for an individual as well as society, create justice and harmony and strengthen mind and character of the people. Vices are self destructive, weakening the mind of an individual that loses the strength and spirit of doing good. The vices are sickening and make the people vicious, wicked and unkind.

Virtues are healthy emotions and strengthen mind and maintain harmony of actions. The brain and body systems function normally, adding to health and vitality of a person. Vices are sources of disorder of mind, creating disturbed emotions from irrational thoughts, creating either aggression or oppression, weakening mental power, affecting immunity of body, causing disharmony of action.

The divine virtue, love, is blessed to us with life; it radiates and resonates all the virtuous thoughts. The human beings, who reciprocate this love back to divine, receive continued strength of divine blessings, bonding with divine through virtuous thoughts and virtuous actions of their mind. Their impervious faith in divine is rewarded by grace of divine at every step of journey of life. Their resolute devotion and trust in divine upholds earnest hope, confidence and reliance on divine help. Such an honest and sincere divine bonding reaps fruits of virtuous character through divine protection in every circumstance of life as that person is always watched over by the divine, omnipresent, Creator of all. All virtues connect together, consistently maintaining harmony of thought and action for a virtuous life in the secure shield of divine, lighting the way of an individual's life.

You have to run...
The train of your life...
Virtue and vice,
Play seek and hide...
When there is confusion!
To save the life train from collusion,
Moderation is the answer; O, my child.
Then remind your mind...
The vice will drown you,
Virtuous strokes can get you out,
Before, the high tide of your vice.
Pray to the divine...
Keep the honesty of your mind

And see through mind's virtuous eye
You will find the way to ...
Health, happiness and peace in life!

Any individual can build virtuous character by creating awareness of strengths of virtues, gaining knowledge and making the choice of an action by thoughtful deliberations and reasoning as one can broaden understanding by learning righteousness of virtues and errors of vices. A character of your choice has to be your motivation; it has to be in your thoughts, and actions will follow your choice. The vices are errors and your weakness that fail your strength and will of mind. That mind, which does not hold an ill will and is sound and strong, can win will for right action, you decide as that holds strength of virtues, managing balance and order of mind.

Loss of virtues in people has given rise to vices; similarly violence has risen due to decline of peace in minds. Glamour and glory created for violence is accompanied by ascendancy and systematic institutionalization of vices, creating filth of corruption and greed in society, which has become intolerant to virtues. Loss of peace and virtues is personal loss of every individual as there is no escape for anyone from stagnating filth of system we have created. Ascending vices are shrinking room for virtues to survive and life is becoming hard, as people are facing difficulties due to degradation and decline of human mind with loss of virtues, at every step of their life and living.

The vices develop from childhood as secondary nature in people, motivating thinking to respond and act in situations to meet their needs and desires for living, when their interests are threatened. But developing a character with vices is self- destroying as it is against spiritual development of a human being that holds key to individual's wholesome life. No one appreciates and wants to hold on vices through the pleasure of will but people cling to vices due to weak will power and an easy way out to meet their requirements. Vices are weaknesses and imperfections of human character, which lead a person to become vicious and malicious character.

Virtue is nature of soul that has natural love for all creation and it creates virtuous tendency in every human mind. Since equivalent negative force is playing on us all the time, our mind deflects towards vice at moment of weakness. We can see this in every newly born child who is pure and divine, he has no ill will, no malice and free of all vice. As his appetite grows and feelings get wild, he tries to emulate other humans, without knowing their character, virtue and vice, strengths and weaknesses of the emotions, which are built over time...

Ground for vices lay in situations of helplessness and weakness of mind. Under fear, a child refrains from telling the truth, as he fears punishment for honesty shown in telling his acts, which he was told were not right. To escape from the situation, such as intimidation by a group, the child may be lured to another group to seek support without knowing any good or bad about them. There can be number of such situations when mind of a person does not have ill will for the other but gets entrapped into company of people who practice vices. Harboring negative and evil thoughts such as revenge, dishonesty, fear, pride, envy, anger, lust and avarice, etc. make our mind weak and prone to other vices. Some people have terrible habits created due to their mental vices, lack of their self control in eating, drinking and addictions of alcohol, smoking, drugs, gambling, etc.

Best values of humanity

Virtues are best universal value ethics of humanity. They are valuable for individual as well as society. We have to appreciate virtue ethics and cultivate virtues to bring about integration of individual and society that has been increasingly subjected to fragmentation, into self-seeking groups, which deride not only virtues but derail peace, encouraging vice and vicious minds, propagating crime and violence in society.

It is difficult to escape vicious cycle of vices as they degrade minds and weaken will power. We have to make sincere and honest effort to resist vices so as to hold on to virtues. Vices degrade humanity fast, engulfing people into fire of crime and violence, drowning into sickness and misery. The vicious minds compromise for their vice and have brought an environmental decline that cannot be stopped until these minds realize, how far goes loss of virtues and they will pay price of their vice, as misery to whole society will not leave them aside...these irresponsible people have to realize and get out of crime against humanity and let their minds see light of virtues, respecting humanity and life of people and need to preserve environment for all humankind...they need to control their devilish appetites as that is not good even for their own health, only virtuous light can show that to their minds.

Propagation of virtues is the only remedy to weed out corruption, violence and crime from society to save humanity and restore justice and equal rights, respecting right of living for all humankind. Virtues fill mind with love for human kind and respect for all life that is rewarded with integration of self with a glowing health and happiness all the time.

Pass the test of right choice

It's your test every time when you have to choose out of virtue and vice. Remember these points; they will help you with a virtuous choice –

1. Reject violence at every step – thought, mind, language, social interaction and verbal as well as physical behavior.
2. Get out of aggression and anger as early as you can.
3. Fill your conscious with virtuous light (learn about virtues)
4. Disengage your mind with any emotion inside.
5. Check your intention, it should not be maligned.
6. "What is your motive?" ask your mind.
7. Memorize your mind (thoughts inside) its action is karma of life!
8. Remind your mind to purify and keep only virtuous thoughts inside.
9. Be honest with your actions played in life, as your conscious will reflect that back to your mind so that it is not confused next time about your choice and it may become habit of your mind, before you realize.
10. Excess of everything is bad; moderation is advice that will never fail you to climb up the virtuous height, any time.

Emotional detoxification

All psychological, psychosomatic, hormonal and many other

serious illnesses are either directly or indirectly, result of negative emotions and vices. As we know emotions arise out of our interaction with our environment that constitutes our social environment, the people, with whom we live and deal for our living. As per circumstances, corresponding emotions arise, more thoughts play in mind with emotions charging brain that works through body, mind and conscious managing thought exchange resulting into actions and reactions. Each emotional experience of the body and mind along with thoughts is communicated to our conscious, which retains it in memory that is flashed back to mind to remind it and guide, during interactions with the same type of environment or people. Pleasant experiences and positive thoughts strengthen mind whereas unpleasant experiences alerts mind that may cause stress and negativity. All thoughts created from these experiences resurface in mind, which might have been at back of memory in our conscious, even if not shown for a long time. But some people fail to take control of their thoughts and mind, who suffer through prolonged play of negative thoughts and emotions that creates stress on their mind effecting functioning of brain and systems of body which in turn results in malfunctioning of body organs and systemic malfunctioning resulting into different ailments. Prolonged stress creates toxic condition in body that does not allow cure of disease until we de-stress mind so that brain can function normally. Only stress free mind can enable systems of body to regain harmonious functioning and maintain internal harmony and body health.

Emotional detoxification is essential to prevent and cure those diseases that are caused by emotional and mental stress. Understanding emotions and adopting virtuous thinking is first step to build emotional health as toxic state of body is created by prolonged stress of negative emotions and vices. People may suffer through depression or hypertension, if they fail to take control of their thoughts; it further deteriorates their health as disharmony and negativity is created due to inconsistent thoughts that may further cause restlessness and stress in a person's mind. Such person has to work on mind either with help of doctor or through change of environment that can bring a change to mind. New thoughts and environment can uplift the mind strengthening it in no time. A change in thoughts relaxes mind that overcomes stress and rejuvenates health. It strengthens and creates balance of mind that creates positive emotions and let body function normally, creating health and internal harmony. Virtues are healthy because virtuous thoughts are in consistent harmony with action generating pleasure. There is no negativity in mind because virtuous thoughts give no place to ill-will in mind. Anyone suffering from any disease must vouch for virtuous thoughts and a virtuous character.

For a detailed description of emotions, virtues, and vices, please see Wikipedia, and http://www.virtuescience.com/ and
ARISTOTLE'S NICOMACHEAN ETHICS at
http://pages.interlog.com/~girbe/ethics7.html

Virtues integrate peace

Though all virtues promote health, happiness and peace in life; integrity* and silence* are two most significant virtues for creation and integration of peace at all times. You need time for

[1] See page 138, Integration of peace (Ch.- Integration of Humanity).

introspection of mind, for that silence and peace will help with required time and space, which regains its balance, energy and relaxation of mind. A person with integrity and virtuous mind can find all right answers to troubles in life *...

A Guide for Proper Moral Behavior

"Seven sins and seven virtues are listed at http://www.cultureandreligion.com/html/guide_to_moral_behavior.html and these two lists have been aligned so that one set has opposites of other. Here is one presentation.

Seven sins (vices)	Seven virtues
Lust (undesired love)	Chastity (purity)
Gluttony (overindulgence)	Moderation (self-restraint)
Greed (avarice)	Generosity (vigilance)
Sloth (laziness)	Zeal (integrity)
Wrath (anger)	Meekness (composure)
Envy (jealousy)	Charity (giving)
Pride (vanity)	Humility (humbleness)

This combination of vices and virtues seems a simple, rational presentation for defining guide for moral behavior. The goal of this list is obviously, effective integration into human society."

Quotes of virtues and vices

Sincerity and truth are the basis of every virtue.

Confucius

Just as treasures are uncovered from the earth, so virtue appears from good deeds, and wisdom appears from a pure and peaceful mind. To walk safely through the maze of human life, one needs the light of wisdom and the guidance of virtue."

Buddha

Virtue is a habit of the mind, consistent with nature and moderation and reason."

Marcus Tullius Cicero

Patience

Adopt the pace of nature; her secret is patience.

Ralph Waldo Emerson

Patience is waiting. Not passively waiting. That is laziness. But to keep going when the going is hard and slow -- that is patience.

Unknown Source

Patience is a remedy for every sorrow.

Publilius Syrus

Humility

Humility is the solid foundation of all virtues.

Confucius:

Silence

Silence is the sleep that nourishes wisdom. Francis Bacon

Honesty - Integrity

A person is not given integrity. It results from the relentless pursuit of honesty at all times.

Unknown Source

Honesty is the first chapter of the book of wisdom.

Thomas Jefferson

Kindness

Kindness is the golden chain by which society is bound together.

Johann Wolfgang Von Goethe

Be kind to unkind people -- they need it the most.

Unknown Source

Anger

For every minute you remain angry, you give
up sixty seconds of peace of mind.

-- *Ralph Waldo Emerson*

.

Consider how much more you often suffer from your anger and grief, than from those very things for which you are angry and grieved.

-- *Marcus Antonius.*

Violence

The Roots of Violence:
Wealth without work,
Pleasure without conscience,
Knowledge without character,
Commerce without morality,
Science without humanity,
Worship without sacrifice,
Politics without principles.

Mohandas K. Gandhi

Violence does, in truth, recoil upon the violent, and the schemer falls into the pit which he digs for another.

- Sir Arthur Conan Doyle

Power and violence are opposites; where the one rules absolutely, the other is absent. Violence appears where power is in jeopardy, but left to its own course it ends in power's disappearance.

Hannah Arendt

Violence is chaos – first inside mind, later outside mind. Ka Trina.
"Civilization begins with order, grows with freedom and ends with chaos."

Will Durant

Envy

Envy is the most stupid of vices, for there is no single advantage to be gained from it.

- Honore De Balzac

PEACE = *THE RIGHT CHOICE*

Choosing good thoughts is like choosing a healthy seed that sprouts into a healthy shoot, blooming into a beautiful plant, which not only makes you feel good and is an ornament in garden of your life but its pleasant fragrance also pleases senses of others, touching their hearts and minds.

Different people understand differently the meaning and importance of various actions and events happening around their life and society. Every individual is a potent builder of 'Peace' or generator and perpetuator of 'War' as individuals' understanding and perception about life varies as per one's capability to learn and evolve through various stages of life.

How one understands violence, war and peace is what one creates and transmutes with his conscious or unconscious actions— that result from his choice of thoughts while living and interacting through life. A mind has an infinite capability and can create a battlefield anytime, anywhere extending to fiercest of wars...- Making Peace a choice means resisting violence and supporting the propagation of harmony and peace. Peace is invaluable for every life. It is an essential need of every human being for maintaining a harmonious functioning of his body and mind for peaceful and happy life.

War and violence is extension of negative thoughts brooding in maligned conscious causing aggression of the mind that may result into violent actions of the body such as disease inside the body and violent behavior outside. A mind with chaotic thoughts influenced by fear, aggression and violence loses its peace and such mind cannot make the right choice...

Devils have the minds,
Whose conscious is maligned...
They create injustice, fear and terror...
Violence is their evil design,
Their choice is to throw humans to war times.
War and violence...
Destroy peace and harmony of mind...
...throwing life to misery and demise.
It's time to wake up and realize...
Always make peace a choice,
Keep its principles high,
Otherwise peace may get out of your life...
Emotions gobble it up,
Violence on it, prey,
Aggression clouds mind, like clouds gray,
Under these clouds, you may astray.
Peace has energy and vigor...
That shines through the mind,
It lights the way of life,
Don't lose it in violence,
That will take you to the grave,
Your health will betray,
Don't astray from peace,
It is the right choice.
Make peace your way.

Every human being longs for peace and tries to maintain harmony as per his own understanding. Given an option out of 'Health' and 'Disease' everyone will choose Health. Why does everyone have one choice - Health? Because healthy state of the body is the right choice as all of us know only healthy body has energy and vigour to sustain body actions. What's wrong with choosing Disease?Disease triggers war inside body. All systems of body are thrown out of gear stopping their normal functions, causing suppression of various bodily functions. A sick body suffers through pains of violence occurring in the body.

Violence and War are diseases, perpetuating in society where as Peace is reflection of healthy societies with vibrant and wholesome lives lived by people, where equal freedom and social justice usher in happiness for all. The choice is in our hands, one with war and another with peace. We have to know and understand the right choice, one that does well for all, that brings happiness to all and that is the one and only choice, Peace. Choose peace in every walk of life. A culture of creating and promoting peace is through promotion of an understanding to help others to make a right choice – Peace.

People ignore making peace conscious choice. Rising aggression in mind does not let people decide right thought choice. People are unable to understand the consequences of their actions, as their conscious perceives only threat to their living and life from rising violence and injustice prevalent in the society. People, who are struggling for their rights of living, fail to take control of their minds and behavior as they are not left with an option to choose, for their peace, social harmony is the need of the society.

Each individual is a potent builder of 'Peace' or generator and perpetuator of 'War'. Understanding peace and making right choice is of utmost importance. Summary of values of peace is given as under to strengthen and uphold choice of peace in every mind:

- Peace is an essential element that constitutes life.
- It maintains vital power of body.
- It has the power of rejuvenation.
- It is relaxing.
- It creates harmony in life.
- It is healthy.
- It prevents and heals disease.
- It integrates human being individually as well as the whole humanity.
- It inculcates discipline.
- It maintains order and balance in life.
- It helps to build concentration, making you focused.
- It gives contentment.
- It gives freedom of mind.
- It is creative.
- It imparts strength to the body and mind.
- Peace holds equality and justice high.
- Peace helps in spiritual rise.
- Peace creates love and harmony.
- Peace makes people kind.
- Peace creates pleasure and happiness all the time.
- Peace enlightens the mind, evolving it to a new height.

When peace is raised, violence always subsides.
We need to resolve...
Put will of violence on hold...
And decide to make the power of peace bold.
Always remember that idea and peace resolve,
That is more precious than gold,
With that peace for you will unfold...
Radiating thoughts of peace, will bring it back to your fold...

Action connection

Thoughts of pleasure and pain are the prompts for most of our actions. Our actions oscillate between aggressive and subtle reactions of our body. Our mind is guided through its own understanding of life and makes its own thought choice. Pleasure and happiness is the strongest emotion that excites the mind and can mislead us, into the wrong choice of thoughts and actions, until our mind is trained to maintain a balance of thoughts for balanced action and behavior. The best example is children who prefer doing enjoyable activities for long hours until interrupted and forced into other tasks. They learn the importance of other activities later in life. Their minds are trained as they grow and understand to accept the merits of other tasks and learn to dispense and accommodate these activities in their available time.

Acquiring material things brings us happiness. So is satisfaction of emotional connection with others that greatly influences our behavior, actions and thought choices. Development of emotional health in childhood goes a long way and plays an important role in the wholesome health of a developing adult, which determines one's adult personality and behavior.

Somatic – sensory pleasure is as necessary as food to the body. It is the foundation of an individual's emotional health that assures one of the importance of one's own existence and it bonds one individual to another. Strong emotional health in our childhood is like credit in a bank that strengthens our mind as our conscious reflects back pleasant and happy impressions, boosting our minds with positive thoughts and strength throughout life. Weak emotional health during childhood ruins the mental development of children and they become adults with behavior problems ranging from deeply distressed and meek to highly violent. They are unable to manage their behavior, due to imbalance of thoughts in their mind created by disturbed conscious and such mind is unable to steer thoughts to balanced behavior, due to its inability to evaluate peace and violence and it cannot make the right choice.

Different adults practice different behaviors in the family and as a consequence children are confused in understanding what is right? For example elders expect from youngsters, especially children, respect but they do not feel the need to extend the same respect to children and youngsters. We forget that child is an individual human being with full sense and emotions, thoughts and mind, exploring life and making his own observations and judgments and forms impressions in the same way as adults make up their minds. The child, just like any adult, cares to be respected and treated with the same importance as an elder.

Angry parents and teachers showing aggressive and violent behavior, intimidate children, while ordering them to maintain peace.

How is that angry behavior right for creating peace?

Children escape violence (anger) by temporary silence, but their conscious has imprints of anger, intimidation... and children remain quiet, till fear ends.

Little minds learn and imitate aggression that goes to their minds, with their thoughts and imprints of anger and intimidation, with lasting impressions in their conscious. This affects their thought choice later in life, getting peace, through aggression and violence, seems right.

Right actions begin with right thought choice that comes from balanced mind. We should not forget that our actions influence other people's minds and their thought choice. We have to create thoughts of peace consciously, exercising a balance in actions and behavior, as we are responsible for creating peace or violence on other people's minds and affecting their thought choice.

Once for you...
And once for all,
You have to decide,
You make a choice,
Peace!
The choice, for peace in life,
Is the only right choice!
In your behavior,
And actions...
From the beginning of...
Your thoughts,
Every time, pick Peace as your choice

BEHAVIOR MODE

Observable actions of an organism during interactions with the environment and performing various life activities such as eating, walking and playing, etc. are considered behavior. The verbal sounds, facial expressions and all other body actions, expressed as behavior, become habits and are identified with that organism, distinguishing it from other organisms.

Similarly, human behavior, like that of other organisms, is his physical actions which may be voluntary or involuntary, expressed through his verbal and body language, and can be observed as facial expressions, speech and language, during his interaction with other people and the other entities of his immediate environment from waking through eating till sleeping. Through interaction with mind and nervous system, our brain initiates internal physiological activity, in our bodies in response to external sensory stimulations that is expressed through distinct external body actions, observed as behavior, distinguishing each one of us as unique individuals with own habits and characteristics.

Observable action behavior of a person is under control of his mind, as it controls his thoughts that command his actions, including his behavior. Mind is the centre of information processing, where thought communication with conscious prompts a desired behavior, and directs a person to adopt a particular behavior. Different environmental conditioning such as living in different culture will have different thought information and different conditioning of people's minds. Different thought influences result into different behaviors. The mental interaction of people of particular culture will develop same consciousness depicting quite similar behaviors.

A number of other factors, personal (age, attitude, emotions, virtues, genetics, etc.) as well as social (environment, ethics, authority, values, education, etc.) effect thought communication, creating beliefs and desires in individual's mind which in turn influences his behavior.

Civilization has changed natural habitat and environment of human beings and this has changed humans values, creating civilized societies of new material world, replacing humanity in human beings with money, power and material, seeking unending excitement and pleasures. Unconcerned and ignorant about any balance of order in their lives, people are aggressively chasing material, money and power, subjecting their bodies and minds to stress and violence. People, due to disbalance in natural healthy living, are losing harmony of life that is seen in increased aggression of mind and violence prone behavior of people, individually as well as in groups. We are facing violence all around, in family, in communities, in states and belligerent nations aggressively collecting arsenal of warfare and eager to prove their might, indulge into politics of terrorism and wars, pushing this beautiful world towards brink of disaster.

Natural as well as social environment are very important for healthy behavior of people. Ever increasing destruction of natural environment is increasingly affecting our health and we are struggling with host of infections and diseases, caused by disorder in body with unhealthy and weak mind, from negative emotions. Anger, irritation, intolerance, frustration, fear and other negative emotions have great impact on nervous system and brain that result in stress, disturbing physiological functioning of all systems of body effecting health and behavior of people.

Aggression is a natural phenomenon in predatory animals to get food and to enhance the mind's alertness and the body's strength for desired actions as natural reaction, by body's defense mechanism. It is a natural response to perceived situation signaled by the stimulus generated through nerves of sensory organs such as eyes, ears, nose and skin that interact with environment and brain to initiate emotional and physiological reactions to propel mind and body into desired state, an enhanced state of strength and preparedness to enact the required behavior. This natural aggression is probably a boon to enhance efficiency of mind and body, but unfortunately it is being channelled into violence in human beings and heinous crimes are committed due to violence prone behavior which creates fear, hurts the conscious and minds of one and all.

An act of violence is committed with intent of intimidation, disruption and destruction, irrespective of cause. Violence and aggression initiate thought interaction with the conscious of other people and initiates action in minds, signaling threat and fear that creates further violence and aggression in these minds, as challenged mind react for self defense. An individual's violent behavior is as much destructive to himself as is to others. Apart from individual violence in society, with ever increasing crimes, there exists structural violence that is carried out systematically by vested interests against groups of people in society through misuse of law and abuse of power, creating hell on earth, through corruption of minds. When people are cheated, their conscious knows and their behavior is influenced through their conscious interaction with their mind that guides behavior accordingly...

Emotions are feelings associated with physiological state of body, influencing our brain and mind attention, motivating thought and behavior activity, creating peace or violence through our actions. An unsound and untrained mind is unable to control aggression and negative emotions and therefore, they greatly affect behavior and health of such persons. We must learn to observe and balance our emotions as these exercise greatest influence not only on our behavior and health, but our social environment and interaction with others too, which in turn affects their behavior. Emotions are like elixir in the body; it is required to limit it in the correct balance for healthy behavior. Mind conditioned with virtuous thoughts gains strength to control emotional balance bringing along balance in behavior.

We have to make conscious efforts to train minds into the habit of peaceful thought choice for appreciable peaceful behavior. The principle, "Think before you speak" for verbal behavior, also goes for appreciable physical behavior, we should act thoughtfully to check aggression and violent acts. Training mind to keep it cool before beginning any action and take time to think and act peacefully, will help exhibit balanced behavior. Children need careful parental guidance to help them train their minds, to inculcate appreciable social behavior, at least till age of adolescence, while they are still trying to understand their own body reaction such as emotions and reactions of their minds adjusting to social environment and society. Importance of health, virtues and non- violence has to be part of child education, from childhood creating a right family environment for mother and child, where family members should demonstrate ethical behavior, promoting love and peace.

Social environment of any society needs attention of one and all, as actions of each of us influence interaction, individually as well as between groups in society. For maintaining social order, we need to abide by certain discipline of behavior conducive to maintaining social harmony. Different societies have been created with different cultures, languages, religions with different understanding of different life values, created for social order. The values such as political, economic and cultural values, etc. have been useful for creating social order, but on the other hand, the same values have created wide disparities amongst people creating hatred and violent behaviors. Vested interests manipulate people through these divisive social values, through selective elimination of people from jobs, unequal distribution of materials and infrastructure that results in deprivation, negative altruism, intimidation, coercion, fear, and many other factors that badly effect people's lives, throwing their minds and life out of balance. People thrown into such helpless situation are unable to take control of their aggression and angry emotions, creating violence prone behavior as they are forced to struggle for the bare necessities of life.

To promote peaceful behavior in people, there has to exist individual as well as social responsibility. Authorities as well as people have to work for values that create an environment conducive to peaceful behavior in people. We need to take steps to create uniform social values to promote a healthy social environment, where justice promotes cooperation and congenial atmosphere, creating goodwill amongst all people, keeping minds at peace. Strengthening ethics in society and promoting virtuous character are the only universal social values that can integrate people into a harmonious society, where people can live together in peace.

Verbal behavior is an index of an individual's state of mind reflecting his thoughts that are presented in a language that is vocalized as speech. Our understanding of language is very important for better verbal behavior, as that affects our interaction with others and in turn affects behaviors. A good understanding of any language is essential as words have versatile meanings, affecting communication, interaction and understanding among people that influences mind and behavior of people. We should observe a virtuous moral code of conduct and abide by those rules of speech and action, which do not result in a negative reaction (violence, hatred, distress or revenge) from hitting out against hurtful words and actions.

The importance of social ethics as well as individual integrity cannot be ignored as they affect the behavior of people and peace in society. This is how our behavior affects our own as well as other people's life. Peace values and other virtues should be practiced and promoted that cultivate peaceful behavior. Effects of peaceful or aggressive and violent behavior are so strong on our health that we must make peace a conscious choice and encourage people to practice peace values.

We can train dogs well in spite of limitations of human to animal communication. It should not be difficult to train civilized human minds, for better behavior in today's organized social system. We need to clean our mind of negative thoughts and feed our conscious with positive thoughts. According to the law of cause and effect, we should try to eliminate any cause of violent behavior, factors that work against peace, for example, controlling our aggression, anger, emotions, language, actions, etc. Thinking before we speak or act, may help to control our behavior as that will help to check unnecessary provocation to the other person's mind. We must consider adapting our behavior in light of this law of cause and effect.

Hints for Peaceful Behavior

Some important 'hints for peace creation' have been given to guide peaceful behavior. These hints are given to create a guideline for understanding your own thoughts and mind in developing balanced behavior that can be helpful in achieving peaceful behavior and creating peace in society. These are valuable hints for an individual as well as a group; to self examine process of thought and action connection of mind, in helping a peaceful thought choice which will act as a guide to peaceful behavior.

Hints for Peace creation

1. Faith – Peace
2. Truth – Peace
3. Choice – Peace
4. Decision – Peace
5. Promote – Peace
6. Attention - Peace
7. Intention - peaceful
8. Attitude – peaceful
9. Behavior - peaceful
10. Responsible - for own behavior
11. Silence – practice it.
12. Non-violence – follow it.
13. Patience – keep it.
14. Tolerance – will reward you.
15. Aggression – control it.
16. Empathize – with others.
17. Conscious – Observe and clean it.

18. Thoughts - screen them and retain only peaceful and positive thoughts.
19. Mind - relax it.
20. Focus - on speech.
21. Listen – carefully.
22. Understanding – expand it – learn "Peace Formula"
23. Benefit – peaceful behavior gives health and happiness along with peace in life.
24. Reminder – its O.K. to fail, Try better behavior next time.
25. Healing action - be sorry for bad behavior and behave better next time.
26. Conflict – solve it peacefully.
27. Give - love, happiness, appreciation, sympathy –(what you can take back)
28. Violence – Reject it.
29. Possible - peaceful behavior, control of aggression of mind

According to the teachings of Buddha:-If every time we feel irritated, annoyed, thwarted, outraged, or just plain frustrated, we reflect on the consequences of our thoughts, words and actions, perhaps that reflection in itself will help to lead us to behave in a way that will contribute to peace...

Mind your behavior. It is an action of your own mind. It creates peace or violence around your life. Your life is your responsibility and it's your duty to create peace in your life. If you want health and happiness with the destiny of your choice, you have to create peace in your behavior and life.

War or Peace
Run the action of life...
A mind, high on...
Aggression
Creates disease and disorder...
Around every life'
Peace,
Is lost into violence and fight'
Losing harmony and happiness in life,
Violence,
In your behavior is...
The action of your will and be the karma of your life,
And your...
Behavior,
Creates the way to the destiny of your life!

* * *

ARISE PEACE TO HEAL

Escalated violence in individual behavior and society is bothering people, affecting living, disrupting the harmony of nature and life. Disorder in society has set on destructive, violent actions throwing the future of society into uncertainty. Thoughts perpetuating violence make the conscious sick of war and crime. The human body, unable to handle this violence of mind and environmental decline, is slipping into disease and behavior full of violence and crime. Not only are our bodies are sick and brains have disease but also violent thoughts have destabilized the mind and humans are destroying nature and animal life....people are sick with fear upon seeing violent violence on violent rise.

Health is not possible without peace as health beholds the same values as peace. The seat of creation of peace and health is the same, the mind. All components of peace influence the health and healthy living of an individual. How important is peace for building our health and role of aggression and violence in creating sickness and disease is explained next.

PEACE AND HEALTH

"The body is a big sagacity, a plurality with one sense, a war and a peace, a flock and a shephard."

–Friedrich Nietzsche

Creation comes alive through Mother Nature. The universe (Macrocosm) is constituted of five elements (Microcosm), Ether, Air, Fire, Water and Earth that constitute life on earth, so are we, part of nature. Ayurveda, oldest system of medicine that believed in 'Natural Healing', is fundamentally based on the principle of similarity between macrocosm and microcosm. Five cosmic elements are considered as subtle matter states or energy that is interchangeable.

Peace is the first constituent element of the creation of Mother Nature that is ethereal in nature and the all pervading universe.

Peace is energy,
Resource and Nature's mercy...
Spreads through the Ether,
Blows with the Air,
Charged by the Sun,
Flows with the Water,
Sprouts into life,
In the 'womb of the nature'
Lives on the Earth,
From life to life,
Lost in the violence,
When you are healthy and fine,
Peace resonates in mind.

Peace is the first of five elements, 'Ether' or 'Aakash tatva', which constitute life. It holds together and gives space to other four elements, Sun, Air, Water and Earth composing universe. Peace is the all-pervasive divine power holding creation alive. It exists everywhere, in any form of matter and energy. Its nature is ethereal, always giving space and power to others. Perfect peace is a form of divine love that is always carried by spirit and can only be realized by spiritual awakening and devotion to the divine.

Peace is not only an essential element of life but also a force of integration to maintain individual as well as social harmony that maintains social order with a healthy life. It is supreme positive force of subtle energy that balances all natural negative energies on the planet, strengthening the stability and equilibrium of life. Peace, being a component of life, is vitally important for the functioning of the body system, maintaining harmony inside the body, which is essential to manage health at all levels. Creation of social peace and health should matter to all people as that is important for all individuals, to maintain their own health as well as peace for living.

All five elements have to be in essential balance of order to maintain life. Any imbalance in the order of life elements, brings disease to living beings and destruction to the environment. Our body suffers continuous decline in health until the elements of life are brought back to the order of balance through appropriate remedies. Therefore maintenance of peace, the first element, is of utmost importance for healthy humans and humanity.

Optimum health of body is not just the mere absence of disease, but also harmonious functioning of organs and systems, as well as spiritual health and balanced mind that is capable of managing healthy social interaction creating peace and goodwill through healthy and peaceful behavior. A healthy individual has a sound mind with harmony of thought and action exhibiting peaceful behavior, maintaining social harmony as peace and health reciprocate each other. Persons who are not peaceful cannot be healthy and sick people cannot be at peace as they lack internal harmony and balance of mind. They lose harmony of thought and action and exhibit irregular behavior disrupting their own environmental peace as well as health and vigor of their body.

Mental health of an individual depends on the state of thoughts of his mind, which creates various emotions effecting brain and nervous system such as fear, anger, excitement, sadness happiness, etc. that create secondary emotions and chain of thoughts with positive or negative feelings, which further effect state of mind and body. It is natural for mind to receive all kinds of thoughts as it is an open ground, receiving different thoughts from all directions and retains thoughts of its own choice, blowing away rejected thoughts. Conscious of an individual, when conditioned with impressions and perceptions of high negativity such as fear, results into emotional distress and behavior of depression or aggression. Prolonged stress and depression create various diseases. Individuals with a maligned conscious spread ill–will amongst people as thoughts of malice, greed, jealousy, hatred, anger and revenge, etc. cause thought unrest, anarchy and violence as other people's conscious perceives these thoughts and their minds are bound to react unconsciously to thought waves received by their subconscious minds. Noble and holy thoughts are generated from pure conscious that does not signal any threat, fear, mischief and any other negative impact to hit well - being of others, and their conscious remains restful maintaining harmony as it does not relay any threat signal of breaking people's peace.

Our body, under stress suffers malfunctioning of organs and systems that generate toxins resulting into various types of diseases. Every single thought vibration has a great impact on each cell and organ of body systems as it communicates through brain effecting chemical and electrical changes that effect anabolic and catabolic reactions, which influence physiology of body. We need to keep our conscious clean and pure to maintain our spiritual health as that keeps mind free of stress that helps our brain and body to function smoothly. For this we need to train our mind to watch and weed out vicious and negative thoughts and feed it with positive and virtuous thoughts.

Detoxification of body as well as mind is necessary to clear toxins and bring them back to a healthy state. We should always make conscious effort to maintain positive thoughts, maintaining harmony of thought and action promoting peace all around. This is meditation for health and peace, healing body and balancing mind for creating optimum health. Peace meditation is important, not only for detoxification of individual's mind and body but also for social spiritual uplifting of society. Purification or cleansing of thoughts is as important to spiritual health as pure food to body. As food nourishes body, pure thoughts purify and stabilize mind, evolving conscious to higher level, improving spiritual health that further energizes and strengthens mind.

Why creation of peace and arrest of aggression and violence is necessary for our health? How strong can be effect of angry thoughts on mind, to create violence and break down peace and health? A shocking example of an angry and violent behavior of some men, in a recent road rage of aggressive driving, reminds how lethal can be aggression and anger. Verbal arguments between two persons after a minor car accident led to a heart attack and sudden death of one on the spot. The person who died had kept his cool and was all right after the accident until the other man created violence. He became aggressive, abusive and violent in his behavior. He exuded out so much violence that it shocked the other person, transmitting violence and negativity, which led to a fatal attack of extreme nervous depression and the other person collapsed on the spot. This was a mental reaction on both sides, as one mental state of high and extreme aggression and the other of depression. Under extreme fear the initially calm person could not bear the brutality. Minds on both sides were influenced by violence and both failed to take control of mental states, which shows an increasingly weak state of mind and deteriorating mental health of people due to stress and violence.

This draws attention to importance of peaceful and healthy behavior in people, which can only be developed by inculcating values of peace. Aggression and violence in verbal as well as physical behavior is not only concern of behavior health but mind and the other related diseases too. Behavior also effects internal as well as external harmony of individuals, affecting the mind and wholesome health, which in turn effects behavior too. Social and mental health of each-other is affected by people's behavior, aggression and violence, along with each other's own health.

Behavior of aggression and violence is rising day-by-day, showing an increase of crime and terror all around, with a steep rise in psychosomatic and psychological diseases in people. Such examples of acute mental shock are actually larger social picture of mental health of people on both sides of scale, depression as well as violent aggression. That tells about environmental factors, which disrupt peace and harmony, constantly hitting people's minds and conscious. Acute as well as chronic mental ill health is on rise, which is proved from ever increasing number of people lining up in psychological hospitals, and related disease treatment with neurological - psychosomatic and infectious diseases.

Human was blessed,
With a body and its mind,
To carry out the journey of life.
Pleasures and pains,
Are two friends...
...playing with us all the time.
Disease and health are guides,
Those show us the wrong and the right.
Violence brings disease,
Disease brings pain and violence to the mind.
Peace brings health,
And health gets pleasure and peace of mind.

Aggravation of diseases and healing process for achieving a cure is directly affected by state of mind as single vibration of thought of war or peace can be destroyer or builder of peace or health as that initiates chain of thoughts. All thoughts together have unimaginable impact on our health individually as well as socially. Peaceful and relaxed mind preserves energy where as it loses energy in state of aggression and violence. Peace in mind energizes vital power of body and strengthens its immune system, accelerating healing, where as negative and violent thoughts lower vital power and resistance of body that retards the healing process, causing aggravation of disease. Stress created on the body by negative and aggressive state of mind not only impedes functioning of body system but immune cells and body organs, and creates toxins under stressful physiological functioning that in turn create fertile ground in body for germs to cause number of infectious diseases.

Peaceful thoughts propagate peace and health. Everyone owes to their own health to harbour peaceful thoughts. It is responsibility of all to check any 'war of violence' to give way to 'peace and harmony' to evade disease and work for health respectively. Together, all of us have to create universal peace and universal health, purifying absolute universal conscious with pure and harmonious thoughts and work for healthy humanity and healthy conscious, where people can take control of their minds in peaceful environment.

'Wealth 'of 'Health' is your 'Interest'...
From the 'Bank of Peace'.
Where Health is 'Credited,'
When you Invest Peace.
Disease and violence will debit your 'wealth'!
That is the law of 'Bank of Peace'.

Hippocrates, father of modern medicine wrote, "The natural healing force within each one of us is the greatest force in getting well." Major research work is going on all over the world to find the cure to various diseases, working along this thought, "the natural healing force" and mind – body connection of disease. Various techniques and alternative systems of healing based on above thought line have been developed that are successful in curing a large number of diseases. An individual's thoughts and mind connect him to every aspect of living, including one's own body, action, behavior, and disease. Therefore healing process must connect and get affected with each thought in mind. For curing any illness mental state has to be relaxed and peaceful. Mind should be trained to develop a 'peaceful habit' by exercising control over negative thoughts and developing peaceful behavior so as to check stress of aggression or depression.

Our body is a natural system operating as part of natural creation and laws of nature govern its systems. 'Vital energy force' that is natural force, acts through principles of nature in body of living beings, including human beings First law of nature and creation has to be integration of peace for continued creation. All organisms and systems of nature are supposed to maintain their natural order of balance and harmony in their action so that nature's harmony is not disturbed and life of all living beings goes on in natural order. There must exist a natural deterrent (punishment) for those who break this law. Nature must have inbuilt systems to enforce its laws. Perhaps development of disease in body and violence in society is natural alarm and result of breaking natural harmony and peace of systems. We have to arise peace to restore balance and order in our environment by arising peace in all systems of living and life, including our body, mind and behavior.

Various components of peace are important to be understood for building social and individual health as much as their understanding is important for creation of peace. Conscious of all of us is connected through the collective conscious and so is everyone's health. Our health is affected by each other as our life is effected by social peace and violence. We normally see this, when people catch infections from each other and social ill health is depicted in epidemic proportions of infections just like escalated social violence. Nature does not ignore, it keeps operating its laws to weed out diseased organisms and corrupted systems to restore health and peace. Our mind and body being part of natural system, have to be kept in a healthy balance, maintaining natural harmony in our actions. For that we need to understand our body and mind for living a healthy life. Conscious and thoughts are important for our mental and spiritual health so is importance of our body for healthy mind and healthy behavior that is in turn important for managing our social health.

Mind is centre of action of life but mental health also depends on physical health of our body, therefore we should strive to achieve wholesome health. For building natural health, we have to begin with restoring natural balance of constituent elements that maintain health of organs and order in functioning of body systems. Since peace (Ether) is first subtle element that gets disbalanced the most, it has to be essentially brought back to natural healthy balance. Systematic creation of harmony and peace for our health can be worked around following areas of an individual and his living -

- External harmony, behavior and environmental health
- Internal harmony, mind and body health
- Spiritual health (Integrity and strength of mind)
- Social peace and social health

To understand and create peace, wonderful peace formula* has been given in the book. To create harmony and peace in life, one has to understand peace components and work various factors at individual as well as his social environment. A peaceful behavior can be achieved through peaceful mind, creating harmonious thoughts and actions that not only strengthen mind but also formulates peace at all levels of individual and social living. External as well as internal harmony requires balance of action and harmony in mind so that mental health and peace is maintained. Peaceful habit of mind has to be created for creating mental peace and wholesome health.

---

* See page 70

Habit of mind

Connection of mind with thoughts, conscious, brain and our body is inseparable so is increase in incidence of diseases and building health. We, therefore, should make peace promoting thoughts, a habit of mind, to always keep mind in constant positive, peace and health building communication with body and brain. For instance take simple example of most important virtue of peace — Justice. The virtuous thoughts, promoting justice makes a person kind and respectful to other people's lives and their needs and rights. It goes a long way in creating peace and health for all connected to that environment. If sharing, loving and caring, are made habit of mind that will always make a persons sensitive to do justice to others – in family, society, authority and institutions and for ones own body. Only mind, which is conscious about justice, will be able to do justice to one's own body, as it would be able to see and limit actions in all respects. It will have a strong will_power and manage a balanced eating, drinking, breathing, relaxation, etc., hence judging needs of the body better.

Vices are vicious and can corrupt mind. If vices become mind's habits; you may become addictive to vices for life. When your mind is corrupted and vices are your delight, you take pride in cheating others and corrupting others minds, without realizing that actually you are cheating your own body and mind. You fail to see that your conscious is recording all your lies and your body has to pay price of viciousness of your own mind. Vices create diseases inside body and mind, as body is unable to manage normal healthy functioning with poisoning of toxic vice. You are responsible for vitiating social environment, through vices and corrupting other people's minds.

Make peace, habit of mind to live happy and healthy life. You have to keep your mind kind, to keep peace in your behavior and life, to build health for all times. Therefore it should be always remembered that values of peace are values for healthy and peaceful life and we should always make peace a choice, to keep our own health good.

Peace will enrich you,
With 'wealth of health',
Throughout your life...
Let peace prevail, and life rejuvenate.
Your health can only stay,
In a peaceful mental state!
Make peace a "habit of your mind",
That will keep health and happiness in your stride.

Most of diseases and their symptoms appearing in our body, can be due to stressful action in mind. We see and feel only physical symptoms therefore we understand and care about our physical health only, but we have to realize that mind and body emulate each other and actions (including disease) are replica of one another's state of health—perhaps just as matter and energy change into each other in physical world in nature, action and interaction of mind is exhibited through functioning of body. Our emotions and thoughts align through mind with body in such a manner that they together can be called 'mental function'. This mental function is the turning point of every action of human life, including health and disease. A peaceful mind is indispensable to maintain natural health and vigor of body that means health is achived at all levels of individual interactions through mind as well as body.

Though segregation of health at different levels cannot happen, but health is generally classified as follows:

- Mental health
- Physical health
- Behavior health
- Spiritual heath
- Social health

Our behavior and overall physical health of our body exhibits first signs of disease, which can be observed and cared for by knowing body and its systemic functioning at various levels. Various body organs and their functioning is classified according to nature of work as under:

Lymphatic/Immune System: Lymph, lymph nodes and vessels, white blood cells, T- and B- cells are major organs, which manage immune system of body.

Endocrine System: Hypothalamus, pituitary, thyroid, pancreas and adrenal glands secrete endocrine hormones, which act as chemical messengers of body and help to regulate physiological.

Nervous System: Brain, spinal cord and peripheral nerves together coordinate functioning of all systems in body, including behavior.

Circulatory System: Heart, blood vessels and blood together manage transportation of various nutrients, chemicals, hormones and gases from and to various organs.

Respiratory System: Nose, trachea and lungs are main organs of respiration that helps in gaseous exchange (oxygen and carbon dioxide) of body to purify blood.

Muscular System: Skeletal muscles and smooth muscles throughout body that provide movement in various organs and skeleton system.

Digestive System: Mouth, esophagus, stomach, small and large intestines are main organs that carry out digestion and assimilation of food.

Excretory system:

(a) Urinary System: Kidneys, ureters, bladder and urethra are main organs that help in excretion of liquid waste from body. These organs filter out extra water and toxins that need to be thrown out of body.

(b) Last end of alimentary canal, large intestine and colon throw out solid waste out of body, through anus.

(c) Skin throws out extra salt and water through sweat.

Skeletal System: Bones, cartilage, tendons and ligaments provide support and protection to various organs of body.

Reproductive System: Ovaries, oviducts, uterus, vagina and mammary glands (female organs) and testes, seminal vesicles and penis (male organs) are reproductive organs that allow activity of reproduction, sex determination and related functions in female and male body respectively

A brief introduction of human body organs and important functions of each system, given above explain importance of each organ and system of body in maintaining health of an individual. All systems are interconnected and interdependent, while doing their specific jobs. If one system is not functioning properly, all other organs and systems are affected.

As internal organs and their functioning are interconnected and interdependent so is our wholesome health, affected by unhealthy state of individual at one or other level. Physical health effects mental health and vice versa, both effecting our behavior and social health, whereas spiritual neglect effects our health at all other levels, as an ill body, which is unclean cannot behold spiritual health. Without healthy purification of individual's body and mind, wholesome health is not possible.

Apart from sudden shock and accidental deaths from an aggressive and violent behavior, it immensely affects our health in day-to-day life, compounded by stressful life and polluted environment. Stress affects our brain with adverse effects on memory, concentration and learning. Stress, whether acute or chronic, effects physiological functioning of various systems and causes various diseases in mind as well as body.

You can look for various signs of stress as given at -http://www.medicinenet.com/stress_and_heart_disease/page2.htm and take care to relax to escape various stress-related diseases.

Physical signs

Dizziness, general aches and pains, teeth grinding, jaws clenching, headache, indigestion, muscle tension, difficulty sleeping, racing heart, ringing in ears, stooped posture, sweaty palms, tiredness, exhaustion, trembling, weight gain or loss, upset stomach.

Mental signs

Constant worry, difficulty in making decisions, forgetfulness, inability to concentrate, lack of creativity, loss of humor sense, poor memory

Emotional signs

Anger, anxiety, crying, depression, feeling powerless, frequent mood swings, irritability, loneliness, negative thinking, nervousness, sadness

Behavioral signs

Bossiness, compulsive eating, critical attitude of others, explosive actions, frequent job changes, impulsive actions, increased use of alcohol or drugs, withdrawal from relationships or social situations

There are a number of acute and chronic diseases, infections, psychological and psychosomatic diseases that result from mental stress, viz :

- All types of pains, anxiety, depression and tension for example-headache and other body pains, insomnia, psychological diseases.
- Heart, high blood pressure, coronary heart disease, Ischemic heart disease etc.
- Stomach and intestine diseases, indigestion, ulcers, constipation, etc.
- Respiration, asthma, infections diseases

- Brain and nervous system diseases – Psychoneuroses, Insomnia
- Hormone imbalance, women's as menopausal diseases
- Immunity related, Infections, skin conditions, such as eczema
- Chronic, obesity, diabetes, tinnitus, sinusitis etc.
- Behavior related- Nervousness, depression
- Addictions – Alcoholism, smoking, drugs, food addictions

Doctors, when treating patients, begin with history of disease, but this cannot be separated from life history of the patient, as he lives his life through body and mind- and the two, interact with environment, all the time. Detailed life history of living of patient is of utmost importance to understand his disease and to take remedial action to cure it completely. Lifestyle based on natural healthy living is bio-social science, of living healthy life. All health care and cure programs should work through patient's life style and his natural living, to prevent and cure disease and recuperation of healthy body. It is not possible to work through any complete cure and healing of patient without his understanding and active participation, mentally as well as physically, as it requires, one's own individual attention and care of body. Besides medical help individual has to mind his body, his health and his living just like his own behavior.

Just like creation of peace, action of health and cure has to go through mind, as it cannot be separated from basic actions and causes that produce disease in body. For better understanding, cure and control of disease, bio-psycho-social model will not only be ideal for attaining health but also for creation of peace as it is through our behavior that we create peace or enact violence that is 'mental function' governed by mind. This is science of building health and also building peace, which is also science of preventing violence and disease.

This science of health and peace...
Does not cease!... with violence and disease.
Peace builds health...
A peaceful behavior, balances mind with peace,
Tell your mind to remind and remind...
The feast of health and peace will be a human and humanity feat.

Keep arising health that will arise peace...tell your mind to ride your behavior, with a virtuous leash and a kind tweet...

Arise peace to heal the body and mind.
Arise peace to turn the behavior kind,
Arise peace to free people of fear and crime,
Arise peace to take on violence and its violent rise,
Arise peace in the thoughts and violence will subside,
Arise peace to drain the brain of disease and pain,
Arise peace and violence will fail,
Arise peace to keep the life on rail,
In the harmony of Nature, a healthy human will sail.

Our conscious has been attacked repeatedly by lies, hate, cheating, terror, deprivation and injustice... It has been loaded with fear, insecurity and uncertainty in life. It has lost strength of trust and faith, as no one seems kind. Vices are overshadowing virtues and souls will die and violence will end life, with war and crime...

Arise peace to heal the conscious in every life.
Arise peace to end strife of vices and violence in life.
Arise peace to create virtuous life.

Society is brooding injustice, corruption and crime, as people with vices have sick minds. They cannot see, distinguish between right and wrong! The vicious minds fail to see rise of social crime and violence getting back to them with disease to their bodies and sorrows in life...

Arise peace to heal the social strife,
Arise peace to make a right choice,
Arise peace for social justice, and life will be fine.

Our institutions are no longer sacred due to corruption of mind and unkind humans, bringing misery and pain to people's lives. Painful is humanity's plight, people suffer from hunger and have no place to sleep at night. Inequality in human life tells tales of wicked minds, who are perpetuating violence and terror on humanity that will destroy this planet and its life.

Arise peace to heal humanity nationwide,
Arise peace and keep its principles high,
Arise peace and heal the humanity worldwide,
Arise peace for freedom and social justice,
Arise peace so the people can live with equal rights,
Arise peace for people's rights that is every nation's pride.

Nature is losing its natural environment fast and harmony of life cannot last. We have to save Nature and to escape rising violence; peace must be given its place. That will be time, when souls will be in solace, tranquility will be in minds and each human will be in health's grace and smiles will light every face.

FAMILY FOR HUMANITY

Man is a social animal and dwells in groups and communies together with other individuals. It is natural need for him for preserving human species. Generally speaking, family is group of male and female individuals of common inheritance or others who get married into family and their family members, who share living together in one house or more. Family is expected to be conducive to every member's happy and healthy living whereby everyone is able to progress and gain stability with a steady support from family members. Individual relationships in family keep changing with varying roles and responsibilities. A family is created under an understanding of sharing and caring for each other. Individuals are supposed to live with certain sets of rules, generally senior adults act as role models, as per culture and religion in traditional families.

A family is typically defined at thefreedictionary.com – "A fundamental social group in society typically consisting of one or two parents and their children. Two or more people who share goals and values, have long-term commitments to one another, and reside usually in the same dwelling place. All the members of a household live under one roof."

Family defined by Wikipedia - "Contemporary society generally views family as a haven from the world, supplying absolute fulfillment. The family is considered to encourage "intimacy, love and trust where individuals may escape the competition of dehumanizing forces in modern society"[13], and providing love and protection from the rough and tumble industrialized world, and as a place where warmth, tenderness and understanding can be expected from a loving mother, and protection from the world can be expected from the father."

I understand that a family is 'whole family', where a group of people together, constitute a common dwelling arrangement and contribute resources, time and share responsibility along with sharing and caring for each other's life. A family is inhabited by different individuals, complete with varying stages of life, from a child to an old adult (grandparents) - males and females living life together, sharing experiences of life. A family is blessing from God, to family members, to accomplish his plans. It is His way to teach us about life and importance of all human beings and other creatures in life. A family is a school where lessons of humanity are taught, to love and respect all living beings and value their rights of living so as to preserve this beautiful creation. The individuals, together in family can learn sharing and caring for all, equal respect for freedom and justice for all. Family offers a platform for sharing pleasure and pains of life, in secure shelter of love and faith, where all individuals can bloom into prosperity in healthy and happy environment. An equal love for all can ideally be taught in family institution where various relationships and various stages of life together make complete learning. Learning sharing and caring is important not only for sake of human beings but also to understand creation and preservation of other animal species, our resources and environment as they fulfill our needs and those must be preserved and shared by all.

Unfortunately we have disregarded the divine family plan and broken families have become norm of society. As individual ethical behavior is getting degraded, exploitation and torture of weaker have become common in the families. Shelter and support provided by family was strength of individuals that promoted integration and welfare of all family members, therefore love and faith bonded family members together with unshaken trust amongst each other. But today some individuals are increasingly acting under influence of greed for money and do not hesitate to infringe upon other family member's rights. Conniving family members can throw you out of house instead of providing shelter. A culture of protection and welfare, of all in family, has been replaced, by intolerance and jealousy, resulting in exploitation and torture of weaker individuals, mostly women and children. It is almost regular and accepted norm by families where crooked and shrewd individuals play tricks and distort truth for their benefit and ego satisfaction. Some family members do not hesitate in subjecting others to any amount of humiliation, character assassination, and creating obstacles on all fronts of life to curtail other's progress and happiness.

Families are rampant with injustice and unequal living conditions of family members. Heart rending stories of individual torture, sexual abuse and exploitation, where some individuals are forced to work hard as bonded labors and others live life as kings, reveal a trail of degradation of humanity. Heinous crimes such as rape, burning brides for greed of money are glaring examples of murdering humans and humanity. Abuse of women is so rampant in families that it has led to systematic social exploitation of women by men for lust and greed. Discrimination against females makes them weak and unhealthy mothers and children borne by them can never be healthy and hence sick societies are developing, with unhealthy human beings. Women suffering from torture and abuse are unable to provide children with healthy environment and such children start life in negative environment of fear and resentment from inside mother's womb itself. When grown up, these children follow adults and unjust system of family that creates society based on foundation of injustice and violence.

Perhaps Tagore rightly characterized modern civilization as being "masculine" since it is aggressive and insensitive like man. Authoritarian and arrogant men have created demonic society by raising men to position of dominance and power in families and same equation has raised masculine civilization through unfair practices and exploitation of women. But unfortunately it lacked foresight, as this has not only weakened women but men themselves. Younger and weaker males, when depend on mercy of devils of family, suffer equal exploitation along with mothers, daughters and wives, left vulnerable with bleak future, making them bitter and violent with revenge or they lose lives in depression and misery.

Devils in the Family

God sends angels to us as his blessings. But selfish individuals, blinded with lust and greed for money and power, create devils on earth. Our world is full of true stories of angels and devils in every other family. Angels bear brunt of devils so as to save innocent in family. Murder of angel Rama, in broad daylight is shocking and true tale of torture and creation of devils in a family. Driven by greed for money and property, devils of the family did not let him live in peace in lifetime and he had to depart from this world untimely because he was killed by his own paternal uncle, a devil created by the family.

Perhaps story of Rama – the angel, begins before he was born.

This story starts with torture of a woman by men in reputed patriarchal family where authoritarian men ruled, intimidating women. As if men's torture wasn't enough, other women in house also subjected one women to humiliation.

Why, in spite of being most beautiful and hardworking, in the family, she underwent humiliation and torture?

Giving birth to daughters was her crime, whereas other women, in this big joint family, were proud mothers of sons.

Perhaps an angel watched torture of the woman and discrimination with girls.

As savior the angel came on this earth. To save this mother from torture, a son – Rama was born in family. He was most beautiful, innocent and adorable child, who was loved by all and brought happiness to family.

This did not last very long as greed for property and money blinds devil minds, hunger for money overpowers them, as devil's appetites are never satisfied. As Rama was growing up devil minds were working against him to grab his share of property that he would inherit. Intimidation of family and exercise of threat to Rama's life by the devils, continued until he was murdered.

This is a story of devils and one family crime that leaves a trail of questions behind. This tarnished reputation of family (exposing the devils), only that was on other devils minds. As loss of angel brought misery to every family members life and those who still were humane asked each other, following questions many times...

Why it happened?
How it happened?
How could he do this to his own blood?

All in family should look into their mind...as any one of them could be another Rama...who may meet same fate as Devils will not wait to satiate their appetites, which keeps growing with their hate...they do not care for others fate...their eyes search for the next one... who should they slay?

Was murderer a born devil?
Was it lonely act of crime by killer?
Why others, around didn't stop killer from enacting this crime?

No amount of investigation is enough until those individuals who created the devil and connived in the criminal act scan their own conscious and weed out devilish thoughts from their minds.

Perhaps fascism in families create such devils, whose dehumanization and demonization start much before such crimes are enacted, when behavior of all such people goes unchecked due to lack of will, understanding and responsibility in families and communities...

A patronage to these devils - by law enforcing agencies encourages and propagates them and demonic behaviors is growing like a curse in society. These devils rule societies through intimidation and violence and that is how we are living in world of violence and crime that is leading towards war and extermination.

This story – "devil in family" is not story of one family or community, it is tip of iceberg of corrupt system that breeds in our civilized society. System of corruption is ensconced firmly in law enforcing agencies and every governing body of state and nation, and on that filth demons, demonic minds are flourishing.

In civilized world, family is natural living setup for newborn child till he grows up. Family is his only environment for socialization until he is grown up and becomes independent and starts socializing outside family. Environment of child depends more on individuals who constitute that family, or we can also say individuals from society, who create families, who can rebuild a society through healthy family environment that would train mind of growing child. It's the time for all to realize and weed out demons from families and society, and take control of own minds so that peace and love may flourish that will create heavenly family times. Virtuous life and the other values of peace are steps to be learned to upkeep justice and love, so virtuous mind would check devilish thoughts and behavior of family members, Thus peace and humanity on earth will shine, when love in families will be revived...

Individual understanding and social responsibility are crucial for healthy development of child into adult as progressive and peaceful citizen; otherwise we may be creating only devils, which will make our life miserable, with violence and crime. Importance of various family relationships lies in family members, honoring their responsibility towards each other. Especially, mother and child should be provided needed support for healthy ethical living. It's unfortunate that most often these relationships out of families play negative role and create behavior and environment of intolerance and jealousy showing discrimination towards other children of family, where as showering favours to own children. This is first seed of social injustice when inequality is created through partiality between future individuals.

Transformation of behaviors is essential to make healthy environment for children in families. Each family member needs to understand that his or her behavior is one's own responsibility. Irresponsible behavior, showing discrimination and intimidation towards weaker family members, creates negativity in conscious and unprecedented impact on behaviors, of all those individuals in family, especially children, including their own children who will together create future society learning discrimination. Vital need of emotional fulfillment for child is best gift that individuals in family can give with kind and balanced behavior, showing love and compassion to all with equal sharing and caring.

Respecting children and youngsters in family is as important as culture to respect senior adults of the family. An individual, at any age or stage deserves appreciation for his ideas and needs to be respected for freedom of expression, valuing his views and honor. That enhances one's self-confidence and draws emotional support to strengthen mind to status of equality and impartiality and that will train mind of child, to appreciate equality, justice and freedom for all humans in their life.

Promotion of individual ethical living is essential to make family truly fulfilling and happy home for all family members, and to further create harmonious society of virtuous individuals who can weed out corruption, injustice and crime from society. Those who are blessed with families, have responsibility to set examples of appreciable and balanced behavior so as to enlighten others with love and compassion equally caring for all in society.

Child is peace,
The life's biggest treat,
In the child, we meet...
The 'Divine' in seat!
Who is the human, kindest of kind,
With the child are humans...
Man or a woman, whose heart is kind,
A caretaker and a mother to the soul divine.
Mother is 'His' honor and 'His' pride.
The man lost his peace, for his misdeeds...
And lost the gifts of his life,
Due to a violent mind, filled, with vicious vice...
Man has to be kind,
Ask to resign, the devil, in his mind...
Revive the family with...
A kind heart and virtuous mind...
Family will then be a heaven and the earth will be a paradise.

KARMA AND DESTINY

Life happens by all actions and movements of living beings, through interaction with environment as natural actions of nature. Impact of our actions and reactions is beyond our understanding as we fail to take control of events, occurring in our life without our wishes. How life goes on with pleasant and unpleasant happenings, where we seem to be spectators, as if things keep happening inexplicably. Since we are unable to exercise control over the smallest events of life, we start believing in destiny, which seems out of our reach and we give up our will and do not make much effort to change our life. When destiny is accepted as the only player we don't pay any attention to our actions as we don't see any strength in our actions and leave all actions to destiny, accepting that it has to dictate our life through unknown karma imposed on us.

What are karma and destiny? How do they play with our lives? Our life moves along path of unknown destiny through unknown karma! How true is that? Is it futile to act on our own? Are we not supposed to exercise our mind? Whose life are we living? Why do we have brain and mind? Endless questions stand in face of destiny and karma advocated beyond our reach, playing our lives irrespective of our present actions forcing us to unknown fate and destiny. Should we believe that and forget any action of will and mind?

Mystery of destiny can be understood, as life and creations are open learning grounds for all to learn, through ways of nature, which itself educates about life. We are masters of our life. We live through our actions, which are an understanding and choice of our mind and our conscious is guide of our life. Mind is there with each of us to lead and explore our lives otherwise it would not have been there in its place; each of us might have been wandering like blind man in open space. Our minds decide and choose our actions, which is our karma that defines our destiny and our life. Each of us enact our own karma. Our choice of thought and action is our karma, which is our own choice. Life follows our karma. Perhaps we are thrown into circumstances as per karma of previous life, testing our actions and karma of this life, for determining course of our lives, our conscious is teaching us wrong and right to enable us to create our own destiny. Impact of our actions affects not only our lives but also everyone around us and vice – versa.

Karma is 'our actions' and 'our choice' that determines our destiny, not an unknown power or unknown destiny, that we cannot describe. Whether in life or after death, our karma stays with us and our life follows the consequences. Our karma is recorded in our conscious. Each action of an individual is his karma, his choice of thoughts and actions, which he chooses with freedom of his own will and mind. Every single thought that is approved by our mind, as its choice is 'action of mind'. It initiates further action initiating chain of thoughts that result into our behavior while performing other actions for our living.

Our behavior is major action, which we enact all the time. Our behavior being display of action of our mind is also part of our karma. We are responsible for our 'karma of behavior'. Either call it behavior or karma; it does have a definitive effect on our life. With honesty of mind, if we judge our behavior and want to change it, we have to change our thoughts first so that unwanted thoughts do not become habits of our mind. That is why behavior is so important to accompany us to destiny of life of our choice. If your behavior is right, you can have destiny of your choice.

Mind is seat of all the 'action of life'. Complexity of nature of mind is still a mystery. Connection of mind to brain is beyond any doubt as it has been established by various scientific studies. Probably understanding of mind evolves slowly as brain is also slow to develop from very beginning. Development of brain is speeded up in 7th month of developing baby, when body is 'ready for action. As baby grows and comes to explore world, brain formation is completed and mind gets ready to take control of life action. Mind is guided by inherited conscious and impressions of life that it receives all the time from environment.

Mind of child is pure and divine, that acts independently with freedom of action until interfered and guided by mother, father and other family members, through their actions, colouring his conscious as they like. As conscious is recording all environmental impressions and actions of mind child starts his journey on to guided path. The innocent child, epitome of divine, with unblemished soul gets trapped into roller coaster of life in this world. By the time, child grows into an adult, his mind gets trained to act through conscious coloured with shades of his environment and interactions, while he was still a child.

As child grows to face life independently, unaware of his mental training, he acts through his colored conscious until he learns his own lessons of life. While on his way, living life is not easy as people forming his social environment create conflict and disease taking over body, hardens his struggle for life that may throw mind into disbalance with sickness if he loses peace of mind. Destiny ignores any excuses and makes judgment of his action recorded by his conscious, at all times.

Day begins when you see light...As you grow and gain knowledge... the time you realize truth...you are able to judge action of life...Now you are master of your actions and your thought choice...that will be your karma...and you can determine your destiny and your life.

Destiny is still in your hands and you can change it, if you try to understand your thoughts and action of mind and be honest with actions for karma of your choice. As realization of truth dawns, one's conscious starts evolving. We must amend our actions. We have to purify our mind through purification of its thoughts. We have to pay attention to our thoughts, attitude and actions of mind as body health and behavior action will follow that. We should guide our mind to right action and morality.

Right Action in Buddhist Morality -As cited at : http://online.sfsu.edu/~rone/Buddhism/BUDDHIST%20IDEAS%20FOR%20ATTAINING%20WORLD%20PEACE.htm

"That English word 'morality' has for centuries been associated with God's commandments, fear of God's punishments, hope of God's heavenly rewards. However Buddhist morality is not concerned with obeying commandments at all. 'Right Action' translates samma (right or perfect) kammanta (willed action). Kammanta relates to a law as natural as gravity: Law of Karma, whereby skilful actions automatically conduce to good fortune. By definition, skilful (kusala) action is one that arises from skilful mind state: one free of greed, hatred and delusion. Actions have consequences. Skilful action would (i) attract praise of wise, (ii) conduce to spiritual growth, (iii) help alleviate suffering: one's own and that of others. To act skilfully means to act both with good intent (generosity and kindness) and with understanding. This includes understanding of the person your action relates to. It requires enough awareness to know what action is needed for their benefit."

Each action of our mind creates its habit creating individual character and behavior that guides an individual towards his destiny of life. Our destiny is created by our mind that we have to realize. Our hands remind us to do our karma and they are replication of our brain. Intricate nerve connection, of all parts of hands to brain is almost like an imitation that's why they can act perfectly to brain's creative designs, which are directed by our mind... and are our ***Blessed Hands****.

---

* Hands are 'mirror of life' and always remind they have intelligence and power of mind. They are the marvelous tools of creation, given to man from the Creator. For the perfect coordination of their action and play, hands can be aptly called extension of brain. See the poem Blessed Hands at the end of the book

INTEGRATION OF HUMANITY

HH the Dalai Lama said: Consider the following. We humans are social beings. We come into the world as a result of others' actions. We survive here in dependence on others. Whether we like it or not, there is hardly a moment of our lives when we do not benefit from others' activities. For this reason it is hardly surprising that most of our happiness arises from our relationships with others.

Nature has the ultimate power of enforcing change, the 'master power' to control and regulate environment and life in nature and course of creation and annihilation. The resources and the environment in nature have been created in a way that we remain interdependent and must move towards social integration, and the integration of humanity. Nature revives life and replenishes resources through its law of 'change,' that is the governing process of integration and disintegration, which are working constantly in our life and environment as nature's work. It is applicable at every level of our existence, to our conscious, mind, body, spirit and the development of society and civilization, along with our environment and nature.

Every human being is imperfect, and so is his understanding, until one evolves spiritually and is perfected by divine blessings. These imperfections seem to be the natural plan for each person to keep him moving through action of life and find his own destiny to live life. These imperfections make us interdependent and entice us into integration for perfection and to become whole together. This fact of imperfection and interdependence is seen not only in individual human beings but it is evident in social development too. There is no group of people in society that is perfect and free of its internal social problems. There isn't any nation which can be distinguished from other nations as perfect model and is able to exist free of other nations as all nations face some or other problems such as economy, politics, security, terrorism etc.

All body organs are interdependent on each other's functioning and connect with each other through various pathways, such as Nervous system, Circulatory system, Endocrine system and Sensory system. Similarly all nations connect with each other through people and the social systems catering to their needs. Interdependence encourages integration for well being of all human beings, which is nature's design for well being of humanity. Perhaps imperfections are nature's design to create different identities and variability in life, which created the need and desire to unite and become whole. Interdependence creates bonds of unity and integration that strengthen united humanity.

Our similarities and common interests unite us into one family or group, such as culture, religion and nation. All people in the group think beyond self-interest, for welfare of all in the group. This shows that we, humans are not inherently selfish and have a natural instinct to care about others. Why the same people behave indifferently and act against people of other groups with the same human kind? Why same people become intolerant and hostile towards other people just because they do not belong to identified group? And all around the world, inter - group violent conflicts are corroding humanity into disintegration as if devils created this divide between humankind through their selfish and violent design with their vicious minds to satisfy their own demonic appetites and they mislead people, spreading venom in minds, creating a negative attitude towards others, so they may not unite.

How do positive minds holding positive values for the well being of people for each other in a group change to a negative and evil state of mind, which does not hesitate to act viciously, against the same humankind who is just sitting on the other side? There can be any number of reasons but major conflict arises due to the conscious, which has been evolving around false values that are attached to groups, not human beings. Some vested interests with vicious minds and selfish motives play these values to manipulate people to their self-serving goals and they use tactics to create fear and barriers to keep the human divide alive, between the same human kinds, who may have been just with a different thought type. These vicious people are actually forces of disintegration who create values that go against the integration of humanity. Just a few such people together create a system of exploitation in society and deter people from associating with other groups and human kind, creating hatred and fear psychosis. Fear dominates in life and society, making most people weak and susceptible to exploitation.

The values of people in such groups are transitory and not their strength of mind and character as individuals but that they are identified together for selfish motives and their values keep shifting due to a lack of integrity as an individual human being. We must acknowledge virtues, values of strength and integration for human beings. These values create social justice, peace and integration. These values promote sharing and caring between people. Values of virtues strengthen the mind and will power development of peaceful behavior that is conducive to integration of peace and humanity.

Integration of humanity can only be achieved through strengthening values of peace. It has to be worked at two stages: -

1. Escape violence: - The most important way to escape violence is to control aggressive and violent behavior of people. Since people create violence through their behavior, it has to be controlled through transformation of people's violent behavior into peaceful behavior. A social environment of peace and justice has to be created that is conducive to peace in minds and peaceful behavior and healthy life so that aggression and violence subside.

2. Integration of peace: - Integration of peace, through creation of peace and individual integration, through cultivating individual understanding about peace and importance of peaceful behavior for an individual's healthy life. Since people's interdependence for their living cannot be ignored, following steps in strengthening social peace should be considered essential to build peace in society –
   - Understanding Peace and the value system
   - Education and environment
   - Integration of peace
   - Behavior

Understanding Peace and value system:

Building people's understanding about peace values and peaceful behavior is very important to help them make the right choices that create peace and harmony in their life and other people's life. The simple peace formula given in this book is very helpful in understanding the components and factors that create peace.

A uniform value system of virtue ethics should be appreciated and promoted to strengthen the cause of peace and peaceful behavior.

All individuals and various groups and communities are interdependent and interconnected as per nature's plan (such as through family members and friends) therefore a uniform social value system is essential so that justice and equal rights for all can prevail, that strengthens integration, not division. The values created around groups are false and temporary as they are not for human integration; they are for temporary gain that has its limits and benefit for only limited people.

To evolve and grow people have to change as different individuals have different capabilities and due to limited use of group value system, people disengage from such limited groups and these groups are bound to disintegrate as they are not essentially founded by all people with integrity. Therefore natural law of universal integrity and creating strong human beings with universal value system is only lasting value system of human integrity for promoting integration of humanity. These values of integrity are values of peace and health.

Mother conscious is always vigilant and watches over conscious of all people. Those people who spread hatred and ill will cannot escape with their evil thoughts as Creator has power of balance and knows to deal with any mischief. No one can cheat divine, the creator, seeking own pleasures while throwing others to pain.

Let the values of justice and peace prevail...
Peace is 'love all' and that will never fail
Violence in behavior is pain...

Respect the values of justice,
Values for a peaceful behavior,
We should entail.
These values will win a peaceful social change.

Education and environment

Education system is most important human creation of reservoir of knowledge that has evolved our civilization. It is also important as it has power to control people's minds through guided education and can change social and natural environment.

Civilization has grown together with education to modern times, where by human being has become master of today's world. Wonderful materials and systems of comforts for human pleasure have been created through science and technology so that discomfort doesn't come to him. Today, life seems to be only man's creation, who has thrown a challenge to 'Creator of universe' breaking laws of nature in his pursuit to become master of universe. It won't be contemptuous if we say education is behind this world order, which has created modern civilization.

While seeking pleasures, we have compromised laws of nature creating imbalance in natural life. Education could not guard human minds and hands misusing it to achieve selfish ends by irresponsible use of science and technology and knowledge to manipulate humanity. We have irrationally destroyed natural environment thus, compromising our health for material pleasures. We are responsible for causing severe natural calamities and disasters by throwing nature out of balance. The world now faces severe threat of obliteration with uncertain and uncontrollable environmental changes occurring universally.

Our crazy meddling with nature has not only disbalanced our environment but vital elements of our life. Air, water and earth have become highly polluted and they have become sources of disease for humans as well as other creatures, causing decline of natural health. We are paying the price of our pleasures with our sick bodies and unbalanced minds due to loss of harmony in our environment. Imbalance in our environment has affected our internal harmony, increasing aggression and violence in human behavior, disrupting the entire planet's peace.

Education, which should have been the tool of all round development of human beings, evolving human character and humanity along with society and civilization, has been focused to achieve material generation and possession. This has led to degradation of minds and mostly educated people are lured by greed, lust, power, money, selfishness, etc. People have been lured for possession of materials, disregarding human values for sake of material value. The importance of natural environment has been equally undermined where irresponsible use of science and technology by the educated has led to unprecedented destruction of natural systems and resources. In the prevailing education system individual's mind gets trained only to seek means for the fulfillment of pleasures as majority of student understanding of life gets derailed on road to materialism. Perhaps education is focused to achieve these material means only.

Education adds knowledge to the mind's intelligence but incomplete and guided knowledge influences conscious and wholesome development of the mind is affected. Its evaluation about life and judgments become biased. Human devaluation is the result of misuse and abuse of knowledge. Education does not seem to have made much difference in evolving the human conscious as we see all educated individuals are not free of various kinds of vices and do not always show respect for virtues, equality and justice. Though a system of education has delivered the best results of knowledge in creating a material world for us in good faith to create comforts for the well-being and welfare of human beings, it has served only marketing and production of materials, while raising work force for same. In process we have lost humanity and its values as there is no place for human values in creating and marketing materials. Values of humanity are recognized by only spirit and for that we need to acknowledge and appreciate equal importance of spiritual development of children, in a system of education.

A child is an independent human being with his own conscious that has fully developed intelligence and capable of learning on his own, therefore any school is important in creative learning environment as child explores and learns from his environment. Thoughts of parents and family form his social environment, that leave an impact on the child's mind as their conscious passes on information to him in nature's 'school of womb' and his own conscious records impressions of his environment since the beginning of his life. Family is the first educational institution of an individual, where various family members are teachers. A child learns inequality and injustice from the very beginning in families, as all types of crimes and unethical behavior are rampant even in families where all family members are educated. In an unjust environment all sorts of unethical behaviors by different family members, may become role models for these young minds. Lack of ethics, increasing intolerance, violence and exploitation are first lessons in educated as well as uneducated families. Double standards are adopted by some family members; perhaps they have a devious conscious, as they do not hesitate to discriminate against other children while they take care to protect their own children. Although we can find, fine individuals with exemplary behaviors and high moral characters, always working for betterment of others, they are sadly overridden by those teaching lies, theft, greed, anger, violence...

Apart from families, schools are a platform of social environment, which should undertake to promote ethical behaviors to check the rise of vices in society. A social environment overridden by vices such as discrimination, corruption, exploitation, swindle, theft, greed, lust and lying etc. acts on people's minds hurting their conscious that creates feelings of fear, insecurity and threat to their integrity. Aggression is created in such minds to face threat perceived through their conscious and anger and revenge surface to fight that injustice and discrimination resulting in violent behaviors. Schools can play a greater role in mental training of children for developing a virtuous character that helps them manage better behavior and peaceful environment.

Schools are shamed time and again for overcharging fees, ignoring student welfare, compromising children's safety and not being up to the expected standard presented by schools during admissions. Moreover teachers and principals of many schools have inhumane behaviors, beating children and driving them to death. This makes it even more important for schools to implement peace education, to give training for peaceful behavior to teachers as well as students and create a culture of peace. Any education is devalued, if it cannot evolve the individual's mind and fails to bring change in the behavior of educated people. Unethical and violent behavior inside schools should be totally eradicated as tender minds and behaviors of children are adversely affected, for life.

Education is the foundation of modern civilization and present society. It has influenced development of the individual as well as society. It has played a major role of integration of people into society, directly or indirectly influenced through teaching economics, politics, health and science, along with cultural and creative development. No doubt, knowledge and skills gained by people, through education enhances their confidence and prepare them better for their life but thorough training and lessons of values of humanity and integration of human beings into a united humanity should also be an inseparable part of education so as to nullify the negative impact of divisive forces.

While undertaking social development, education seems to have lagged behind in its role of integrated individual and social development. Educated individuals are better prepared, physically, mentally and socially but they are hardly near being well-rounded and integrated individuals, with few exceptions. Most students seem to have been trapped as links into education skills and employment, where the role of education seems to be shrinking to generate work force.

Since education has succeeded in creating the present civilized world and with reformatory in approach and proactive focus on individual development such as ethics, language, behavior and mind training, education can bring universal integration of humanity through integrated development of children. Early education is the most important learning and it should be holistic for integrated development of individuals promoting values of universal humanity, teaching sharing and caring of all life in nature.

The schools can be 'social families' where grooming of children into an integrated adult can take place alongwith peaceful behaviour training and their orientation into social integration. The schools should be a place where all children can find a just platform to grow and learn in an environment of freedom and neutral language of coaching books that let little minds develop independently, evaluating knowledge of different subjects and their importance with a free mind. For creating 'power of peace' in people, schools should be 'temples of peace,' and 'religion of peace' should be a culture of education.

Instead of teaching histories of wars and throwing little minds into a war of cutthroat competition, schools should teach histories of those who create peace and promote peace. Let each child create his own history, and build the school's history. This can inspire the future children of the school as guides and heroes who evolve to highest peaks, whose minds and actions are supreme.

Integration of peace

The rise of peace can be maintained through integration of peace individually in thoughts, mind, behavior and socially by maintaining and ethical behaviour in our institutions. Honestly working for integration of humanity and peace will make sure that violence may not prevail and humanity is empowered with peace at every stage. The two virtues, Integration and silence being of utmost importance for maintaining peace in life are discussed in detail-

Integration

Integration is the process of unification. Integration of peace is to create harmony in life. It is to build individual integrity and make people live in harmony, uniting all humanity, for common cause, integration and 'peace to all'. Integrity builds strength and stability of actions of an individual adding value to character, principles, attitude and organization. Integration can be achieved by practicing all steps required to be organized and being strong willed to strengthen as a whole, an individual's integration.

From Wikipedia, the free encyclopedia... "Integrity is doing the right thing, especially when no one is watching."

Integrity as a concept has to do with a perceived consistency of actions, values, methods, measures, principles, expectations and outcome....The etymology of the word "integrity" can suggest insight into its use and meaning. It stems from Latin adjective integer (whole, complete). In this context, integrity may comprise personal inner sense of "wholeness" deriving from (say) honesty and consistency of character. As such, one may judge that others "have integrity" to extent that judges whether they behave according to values, beliefs and principles they claim to hold.... In discussions on behavior and morality, one view of property of integrity sees it as virtue of basing actions on an internally-consistent framework of principles....One can describe a person having ethical integrity to extent that everything that that person does or believes: actions, methods, measures and principles — all derive from a single core group of values....Some commentators stress the idea of integrity as personal honesty: acting according to one's beliefs and values at all times. Speaking about integrity can emphasize "wholeness" or "intactness" of moral stance or attitude. Some views of wholeness may also emphasize commitment and authenticity.

Integration of pure thoughts and virtues builds the character of individuals. Purification of thoughts brings about integration of our conscious. A virtuous character is built through the mind, with a pure and integrated conscious. The integration of conscious through purification of thoughts can transform the collective conscious of humanity. Purity of conscious strengthens spiritual interconnection in human beings, uniting together into one-ness, whole humanity. We miss this wholeness and feel incomplete that is driving us unawares towards others trying to connect through emotional and material needs. But all connections developed through needs are unstable and tend to disintegrate with the fulfillment of need until we have strength of mind, backed by integrated thoughts and conscious.

The fragile connections of desires and needs are unending and keep changing, as circumstances never remain the same in constantly changing life and living. Connections with people whom we think as our own and want to hold on forever like material possessions is temporary and bring pain, misery and suffering when their shallowness is exposed. The soul suffers through incompleteness because of false and temporary connections of the needs and emotions of material world. There is only one unbreakable connection that is with 'His' divine conscious 'Creator Himself.' This connection, with divine conscious can only be achieved through pure conscious. Such individuals sail through any upheaval of this world, in Light of Divine with His blessings.

On the way to our own journey of life, we explore and learn. Every bit of information adds to our knowledge and builds our understanding, conditioning our conscious. Integration of virtuous thoughts purifies and strengthens our conscious and evolves it to a higher spiritual level integrating own self to soul. Cosmic integration of humanity is established by collective conscious through every small act of kindness, justice and helping others in whatever manner possible. Integration is a steady route to climb the steepest mountain to hoist the flag of desired victory. Individuals with integrity, who can integrate themselves, together have power to integrate all humanity and reach 'peaks of Mountain of Peace'.

Many people depict a vision of fractured peace. Peace fragmented into plural numbers, classifying and defining into different peaces as if it can be fragmented into various pieces. Peace has to be wholesome as its nature is to become whole. It has the power of integration to maintain its character of integrity to draw to whole. Viewing peace in parts is leaving room for violence and wars. Peace integrates all, so true peace has to be collective peace where peaceful humanity can exist in universal peace. Individuals blessed with true peace cannot stop peace in their minds; it has to spread all around, far from their minds. They cannot satisfy with their inner harmony overlooking state of environmental and social peace for very long, when other people are in pain and unrest around them. Truly peaceful individuals have to work for integration of peace, creating harmony and pursuing ideals and ways in society to build collective peace in all individuals around their environment. The process of peace does not stop at one individual, and has to be a non-stop integration of universal peace, which lay inert under maligned conscious of people who are unaware of it. It has to be awakened from dormant state in everyone's conscious.

Integration of 'universal conscious for peace' is only possible through integration of virtuous and peace creating thoughts. A 'sea of thoughts' exists around us with diversity in thoughts pooling in all the time due to different understanding of people about peace and life in different circumstances, regions, environments, races and societies. Different languages, religions, cultures and different material needs for every individual in different political and economic pressures are serving only short-term interests of the few in limited groups of people, throwing unlimited thoughts of conflict resulting into actions of chaos, with increased aggravation of minds leading people to violence, terror and wars. Diversity brings color to life but life cannot exist without 'light of white'. Purity of white is peace that tranquilizes all minds into restful peace. We have to understand this and make others understand it. We have to purify our thoughts to see humanity in universal peace. We have to adopt universal values of ethics to integrate all human beings into harmonious humanity for universal peace. Together, we have to integrate with thoughts of others that creates peace, as peace to others is true peace for you. Integration of each 'thought for peace', integrates thoughts of 'peace for all' and 'integrity for peace' in individuals will usher in universal peace and prosperity for all humanity.

Integration of the smallest and simplest acts, can generate unlimited strength and power to achieve the cause, of honest goodwill and welfare of all. A simple act of observing silence creates peace not only in your environment but it also makes other people's environment peaceful. If we inculcate a habit of observing regular silence, it can bring integration of peace through culture of silence, as so many incidents of violence are caused through unnecessary provocation of acts of aggressive behavior. Silence gives opportunity to integrate your thoughts bringing mind to a balance enabling to act it in a relaxed and balanced state.

Silence

The nature of silence and non-violence can be equated with the nature of peace and their importance in creation and integration of peace is known to everyone. Silence is the 'mirror of peace' and reflects in every mind-how peaceful is can be this world? Silence is more than presence or absence of sound or speech. Silence is everyone's best friend; you can have one and others will be pleased to have one from you. It is first virtue that connects us truly to inner self and life around us. It is superpower that controls the mind and clears a way to connect it with soul.

The mind and tongue are two cunning evil duos in our body, which can throw us into many troubles. Silence, being a powerful truth manager, keeps the mind and tongue under control. It restrains the tongue and also makes the mind attentive. This not only controls verbal behavior but also makes mind attentive to decide to direct tongue to speak when it is important to speak to strengthen the truth. Silence is not always mute; it can be a powerful mode of communication, which can be more effective than a spoken language, in certain situations.

Silence can be stillness, where nothing is happening or it can exist amidst the loudest of noises. It can expand to infinity or be just miniscule. But even a fraction of silence makes its presence felt. It saves energy and strengthens our body's vital power that enhances health-building activity inside the body. Silence is of utmost importance to the brain and nervous system, since these systems control physiological functioning of the body by regulating functioning of the body's systems. Our mind cannot operate with sense of balance without the required silence that brings it to the state of equilibrium. It will not be wrong to say that silence and nonviolence are two inseparable halves of peace and they are in reach of all individual's hands, they can always create their peace, which is their responsibility.

Silence and violence, both move with thoughts. When the mind is able to exercise control over its thoughts, it has silence of peace, a state of high relaxation of mind, and it can create stillness by stopping all thought movements, enjoying a relaxed mind, an enlightening conscious, in a state of total peace created by silence enveloped all around, erecting a barrier against internal as well as external noises.

Silence! That is a quiet and restful state of mind can also create a highly violent state, causing restlessness to the mind in various people as they plunge into the grip of highly negative thoughts when alone and isolated. There can be individuals who fail to relax and get any peace in silence, as the 'noise of thoughts' becomes loud in the individual's mind, in which negative thoughts overpower weak mind filling 'space of mind' during silence. Such a mind will get relief from his mind's violent thought movements with something like music or another activity of interest that can distract the mind from 'thought war' by stopping noisy thoughts and creating some soothing impact that will help the mind in transition of thoughts from violent and negative to restful and positive mental state, bringing the state of relaxation of mind and later it can further create 'silence of peace' from escaping noisy thoughts.

As minds are in aggression, so seems the environment agitated by noise pollution. Inventions of science have generated so many machines for our comfort and entertainment inside the home, such as the telephone, television, kitchen gadget and washing machine etc as well as outside the home such as transport, construction machinery and generators and various other industries that silence in the environment has become a thing of the past. Loud music blaring out of microphones in social functions and inside the home from entertainment gadgets has become a source of constant noise pollution for people subjecting their minds to constant excitement causing nervous tension and exhausted mind remains in restless state, losing order of balance. Want of silence makes minds restless. Marketing and media have intruded into our life through every possible way, manipulating mind of people through advertising on TV, radio, computer and other means, resulting in the mind's losing space and silence.

We must make a conscious effort to observe silence not only for our own minds but also for others and save the environment from noise pollution for the sake of creation of peace. We must learn to give a break to our minds from the noisy intrusion of media, advertising, music and other sources penetrating silence and our minds' peace. With this people are losing control and their mental balance and this is affecting behaviors also.

Behavior

Our behavior is the most important factor for maintaining individual as well as social peace. It is also important to us as it affects our health and social environment and harmony in life. Behaviors are your own obligation and remember it can open all locks of life.

'Behavior is the key to Peace in life'

In recent times there has been a steep rise in individual and social violence. Demonic wars of terror are getting louder and louder, disarray is being created by demons of society through violent attacks on innocent people. Humanity is left behind in a trail of sorrows and hundreds of people are murdered everyday all over the world. Those who are left behind from their families live in fear, hatred, revenge and anger, getting ready for more violence, which is not their choice but forced by violent struggle to survive for want of adequate resources and help for their living. Life for some becomes a nightmare after losing family members, who were their support and means of living. The demons organizing and instigating this human massacre are enemies of their own children and future generations, who will have to live in a violent world, under fear and threat of violence all the time. Health, happiness and peace are becoming distant dreams.

Every other person is suffering like Jazara and wants to get out of the tribulation of violence and desires peace. Her family members suffered through violence and lived through fear for their life for no fault of their own. Individual as well as group violence is recklessly destroying the quality of life for all people. Those who are responsible for this violent design cannot escape it as their conscious is witness to the actions of their minds. Before the end of their lives they will be judged for their actions and crime against humanity and they will be cursed for their devil actions against humankind and they will have to pay for their sins at the altar of Divine.

My conscious was touched by Jazara's mind, suffering pains of violence. Thought after thought questioned my mind about finding ways to arrest this violence against human kind. My mind seeks an end to this agony and reprehensible behavior of human class, which is perpetuating this violence and war. Day and night, my conscious worked on people's plight, even in my sleep it tried to find, what was wrong and what was right. As clouds of violence cleared, peace was in sight to end people's fright and violence – strife.

Peace is the way, to end violence and fight,
Arise peace in every mind...
Tell the aggression in the mind, to be quiet,
Let peace be your heart's delight,
The violence will end,
You withhold any fight,
Arise and rise peace in your behaviour so the other human is fine,
That will keep humanity in peaceful sight.

When there are more people and more minds, they have to share and care equally and keep behavior peaceful and habits of the mind kind. Elon's behavior was not right, who created violence every time, as he failed to control his mind's aggression. Laqueta did not fight and her behavior was quiet but violence initiated by Elon did not subside until it caused destruction of peace in Laqueta's mind...violent blasts caused by his words, staged a war inside Laqueta's mind...the power of words was infinite as they became volatile with charge of violence from Elon's mind.

"Power of words" should not be undermined; as they can explode the peace of human minds. How much they can hurt tender heart, like Laqueta has described. "Go back to Texas " was not just silent at that time, Elon blasted each word live, making it violent, with aggression filled behavior and his ways were unkind. Elon's aggression with each word was hitting Laqueta's mind that blasted her peace, caused destruction of all bonds of love and faith, with debris of hate left behind...

Language and action of mind is enacted through our behavior, verbal and physical, either creating peace or designing violent strike ... behavior is the language of war or peace...it is capable of generating war or peace any time. The battlefield of war can be only a mind or it can cross boundaries of nation or a class, spreading violence to all-human kind, causing destruction of everything in its sight. Peace flowers in those minds whose behavior is kind and they can create gardens of peace in battlefields ridden with violence and crime.

Behavior of a human is...
An index of his conscious,
And the language of his mind,
That tilts the balance of...
Peace and violence around his life.
It's our behavior that begins and ends any fight.

Peace is our health, giving us life. Without peace humanity cannot survive. Arise and rise peace to keep healthy and fine. Peace is energy save it for your life. Peace accompanies, pleasure and happiness, with health delight for human kind. Humanity shines only in happy and healthy mankind. Humanity in every human is his respect for other life and we have to pass this test of life created for us by the divine. Pass your test keeping habit of your mind kind and integrate humanity by living peaceful life with peaceful behavior and creating harmony in life.

Let us pray together, for the ignorant, who forget HUMANITY and are unable to appreciate others as their equals and have no respect for other's lives... and to uphold their rights, freedom, justice and peace --

May Peace be...
A habit of your mind,
And your behavior kind,
May justice be...
Always in your sight,
May you uphold equal rights!
And respect every life.
May you be blessed with the ...
Peace delight!
Harmony and health prevail in your life!
May you create peace all the time!
Peace may be your happiness and motto of life!
May you stand with peace, holding it high, all the time!

*Blessed Hands**

Hands in prayer, receive blessings divine...
Hands hold the Truth, Faith, Trust & 'His' blessings for life...
Hands are special gifts to human to create infinite...
Hands were gifted to enable us to create on this earth infinitely...
Hands are mind's tools that shape up life,
Hands act for karma and get us destiny of our choice.
Hands get down receiving, teaching humbleness to our mind...
Hands fulfill our needs and make us kind.
Hands are mirrors, showing us way of life...
Hands earn our living...
Hands feed us...
Hands feel and heal the body...
Hands defend us...
Hands share and care...
Hands are friends...
Hands are our strength...
Hands play, the games of life, ...
Hands that hold together high and tight,
Hands lie, in an oath, not to fight.
Hands of friendship, love and peace are their might...
Hands, arise peace to end all strife from every living life...
Hands raised in peace, show the way to mankind
Hands together in Peace may receive blessings divine.

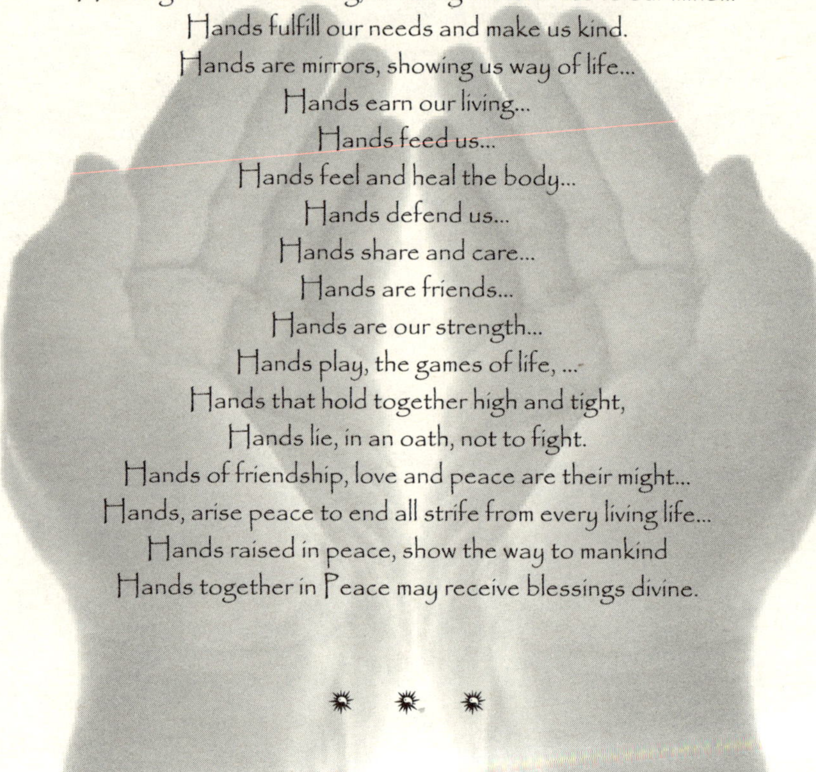

* From page 151